THE SUN AND THE SERPENT

TEMPLE OF BĀSDEO OR BĀSAK NĀG
(VĀSUKI)
BADARIWAR.

THE SUN AND THE SERPENT

A CONTRIBUTION TO THE HISTORY OF SERPENT-WORSHIP

By

C. F. LODHAM

BRIGADE SURGEON, H.M. INDIAN ARMY
MEMBER OF THE ROYAL ASIATIC SOCIETY, ETC.

GYAN

Published by

Gyan Publishing House
5, Ansari Road
Daryaganj, New Delhi-110002
Phone: 011-47034999, 9811692060
E-mail: books@gyanbooks.com

Distribution Network
gyanbooks.com
India, USA, Canada, UK, Australia, France

ISBN : 978-81-212-4551-7 (HB)
First Published, 1905

2nd Impression 2020

Printed at: Gyan Press, Delhi.

The Sun and The Serpent
Author: C. F. Lodham

THE SUN AND THE SERPENT

A CONTRIBUTION TO THE HISTORY OF SERPENT-WORSHIP

By

C. F. OLDHAM

BRIGADE SURGEON, H.M. INDIAN ARMY

MEMBER OF THE ROYAL ASIATIC SOCIETY, ETC

LONDON

ARCHIBALD CONSTABLE & CO LTD

1905

Preface

THIS work, which is based upon papers read before the Royal Asiatic Society in 1901, was, at first, intended to refer only to Indian Serpent-worship. It was soon found, however, that the Serpent-worship of India did not originate in that country, but was, in fact, a branch of the worship of the Sun and the Serpent, which was once well-nigh universal. It became evident, therefore, that a history of the Indian cult would go far to explain the nature and origin of serpent-worship, in other countries and in other times.

It will be seen that some of the views, expressed in this volume, differ from those which have been held by some Oriental scholars of great eminence. These views, however, have not been put forward without due consideration. They are the result of much reflection, observation, and inquiry, combined with a careful study of local tradition and folk-lore. For this, a long residence in India, and an intimate acquaintance with the people, afforded many facilities.

In rendering Indian and other names the popular forms of spelling have been adopted.

The author takes this opportunity to offer his thanks to those friends who have helped him with information or otherwise, especially to Professor A. H. Sayce, whose advice, most kindly given, has saved him from several pitfalls.

Most of the illustrations are from photographs taken by the author.

Contents

CHAPTER I

CONTENTS

PAGES

CONTENTS

CONTENTS

CONTENTS

CONTENTS

CHAPTER VI

CONTENTS

PAGES

CHAPTER IX

CONTENTS

CONTENTS

PAGES

CONTENTS

PAGES

CONTENTS

PAGES

CONTENTS

LIST OF ILLUSTRATIONS

CHAPTER I

THE Nāga, Nāg, or hooded serpent, commonly known as the Cobra, is still held sacred in India, as it once was in many other countries. It is called the good snake, and is considered as a protector and as a harbinger of success.

Although the poison of this serpent is so deadly, few Hindus will injure a Nāga, and still fewer can be induced to kill one.

At many towns, during the festival of the Nāgapanchami, which is held in honour of the serpent demigods, living Cobras were, and probably still are, brought in from the country for sale. These were bought up by the townsfolk, who turned them loose, to free them from captivity, as an act of religious merit.

Over a great part of India the rudely carved representation of a serpent, or a round stone in place of it, is to be found under nearly every large tree. To these Nāgs, as they are called, offerings are made, not of such things as are usually eaten by snakes, but of things suitable for the food of man. Flowers, too, are frequently offered, and lights are burned before the shrines.

It must not be supposed that all snakes are worshipped. The Nāg alone is sacred.

The veneration for this serpent was not borrowed, as some have supposed, from the aboriginal tribes. It is intimately connected with the worship of the Sun, and is thus closely related to the orthodox Hindu religion.

The hooded serpent was, as we shall see later, a totem of the people who claimed descent from the Sun. And the Nāga demigods, who are described in Brahmanical writings as "The Celestial Serpents belonging to Sūrya" (the Sun-god [1]), were deified chiefs of the Solar race.

These demigods belong to a class of deities, no longer orthodox but very popular, which has still its temples, its priests, and its worshippers, both in northern and in southern India.

It is to these ancient deities, rather than to the great gods of the Brahmans, that the Hindu people first turn in times of trouble. To the Nāga they pray for rain for their crops, and to the Nāga, or the Deva, they pay their vows in time of pestilence or famine. To these, also, they offer the first milk of their cows, and the first-fruits of their harvest.

From the Mahābhārata we learn that Swarga,

[1] Paraskara Grihya Sutra, ii. 19. 9.

INTERIOR OF TEMPLE OF BĀSDEO (VĀSUKI),
ASSURI, CHINĀB VALLEY.

the heaven over which Indra ruled, was tenanted by Devas and by Nāgas, with some other divine beings of less importance.[1]

By European writers the Devas are usually called gods, but they and the Nāgas would be more correctly described as demigods. They were deified human beings.

It is necessary to distinguish between the Nāga demigods in heaven and the Nāga people on earth. The former were the deified ancestors of the latter.

The Nāgas are not mentioned under that name in the Veda; but serpents are frequently referred to, as enemies of Indra and the Devas, and are described in connexion with the Asuras or Dasyus.

Some very eminent scholars, following the commentator Sayana, have understood the Asuras, Dasyus, or Serpas, of the Veda, as representing atmospheric phenomena.

The Brahmans consider these enemies of Indra to have been demons, and generally describe them as monsters, with human bodies, but with the heads of various animals.

I hope to be able to show that the Asuras and Serpas of the Rig Veda, the Asuras and Nāgas of Manu and the Mahābhārata, and the Asuras or demons of the Brāhmans, all represent hostile tribes, who opposed the Aryan in-

[1] Mahābhārata, Adi, Astika, p. liii.

vasion. We shall see later that both the Devas, and the Nāgas, or Serpent-gods, are still worshipped as deified heroes.

In the Rig Veda the term Ahi, or serpent,[1] is applied to the Asuras or Dasyus. Thus, in one of the hymns, we find: "With his vast destroying thunderbolt, Indra struck the darkling mutilated Vritra; as the trunks of trees felled by the axe, so lies Ahi prostrate on the earth."[2] Again, it is said: "The waters that delight the minds (of men)[3] flow over him, recumbent on the earth, as a river burst through its broken banks; Ahi has been prostrated beneath the feet of the waters, which Vritra by his might had obstructed."[4]

In another hymn we find: "The strong heaven was rent asunder with fear, at the clamour of that Ahi, when thou, Indra, wast inspirited by drinking the effused (Soma); and thy thunderbolt, in its vigour, struck off the head of Vritra, the obstructor of heaven and earth."[5]

In each of these passages Vritra, who is represented in the Veda as one of the most powerful

[1] Bothlink and Roth, Lex, s.v. *Ahi*.

[2] Rig Veda, I. xxxii. 5.

[3] In these passages from the Rig Veda, the words in parenthesis are supplied by the Commentator.

[4] Rig Veda, I. xxxii. 8.

[5] Ib. I. lii. 10.

enemies of Indra and the Devas, is identified with Ahi or the serpent.

In other hymns, also, Ahi is mentioned as an enemy of the Devas or Āryas. Thus it is said: "To that Indra, the women, the wives of the Devas, addressed their hymns on the destruction of Ahi." [1]

The women referred to in this passage are evidently the wives of the earthly Devas, or Āryas, and not those of the deities.

In another hymn we find: "Mighty wielder of the thunderbolt, when the priests had thus exalted thee (by praise), and the exhilarating Soma juice had been drunk, thou didst expel Ahi from the earth, manifesting thine own sovereignty." [2]

Then we have: "Thou didst perform, O Indra, a glorious deed, when thou didst awaken the sleeping Ahi with thy thunderbolt." [3]

Other hymns contain allusions to Arbuda, who was also a serpent.[4] Thus it is said: "Thou, Indra, hast defended Kutsa, in fatal fight with Sushna; thou hast destroyed Sambara in defence of Atithigva; thou hast trodden with thy foot upon the great Arbuda. From remote times thou wert born for the destruction of oppressors." [5]

[1] Rig Veda, I. lxi. 8.
[2] Ib. I. lxxx. 1.
[3] Ib. I. ciii. 7.
[4] Bothlink and Roth. Lex.
[5] Rig Veda, I. li. 6.

In his remarks upon this passage the commentator, Sayana, says that Kutsa was a rishi, and that Sushna, Sambara, and Arbuda were Asuras.

Arbuda is referred to in other hymns, and there too he is associated with the Asuras and Dasyus. Thus we have: "Invigorated by (the libation of) the exulting Trita, offering thee the Soma, thou hast annihilated Arbuda."[1] And again: "Priests propitiate, by the offering of the Soma, that Indra who slew Urana, displaying ninety-nine arms, and hurled Arbuda down headlong."[2]

Further we find: "Thou hast extirpated Vritra with thy mighty weapons; thou hast been the destroyer of the deceptive Arbuda and Mrigaya; thou hast extricated the cattle from the mountain."[3]

Then too we have: "The thunderbolts of the showerer roared aloud when Indra, friend of man, sought to slay the enemy of mankind. Drinking the Soma, he (Indra) baffled the devices of the guileful Dānava."[4]

In another place we find: "Indra, hero, keep up the strength wherewith thou hast crushed Vritra, the spider-like son of Dānu, and let open

[1] Rig Veda, II. xi. 20.
[2] Ib. II. xiv. 4.
[3] Ib. VIII. iii. 19.
[4] Ib. II, xi. 10.

the light to the Ārya. The Dasyu has been set aside on thy left hand."[1]

Thus we see that Vritra was an Asura, a Dasyu, and a Dānava, and was also of the serpent race of Ahi. It is evident, therefore, that all these were but different designations for the same chief, or for the same people.

In the Sāma Veda we find further proof that the Asuras and Dasyus, Daityas and Dānavas, were hostile tribes. Thus it is said: "O Indra, when fleeing from Vritra Asura's wrath, all the gods, thy friends, deserted thee."[2] And again: "Indra, like a friend, advanced to the front of the battle and slew Vritra. He, like a hero, hewed down the hosts of the Dānavas, and, as a protector, subdued our foes."[3] Then we have: "All the moving tribes of men bow down before the wrath of Indra, as all the rivers bend toward the sea. He strikes off the head of the earth-shaking Vritra, with his rain-causing, hundred spiked vajra" (thunderbolt).[4] And further: "Indra is the devourer of Vritra, overthrower of Bāla, the destroyer of cities, and the shedder of water."[5]

In each of these passages Vritra appears as an Asura warrior.

[1] Rig Veda, II. xi. 18. [2] Sama Veda, Stevenson, I. iv. 2.
[3] Sama Veda, II. v. 22. [4] Ib. II. xvii. 13.
[5] Ib. II. xix. 3.

In the Atharva Veda, also, Vritra is associated with the Asuras and Dasyus. Thus we find "With this talisman Indra slew Vritra; with it he, full of device, destroyed the Asuras."[1]

We have therefore, from the Vedas, ample evidence that the Asuras, Dasyus, Daityas, and Dānavas, who opposed Indra and the Āryas, were tribes of serpent race.

Authorities are not agreed as to who these people were, or whence they came. Let us see if we can trace their origin.

It should be borne in mind that the events referred to in the hymns of the Rig Veda were doubtless spread over a long period, which commenced before the arrival of the Āryas in India.

As shown by Haug,[2] the term Asura corresponds with the Ahura of the Iranians, and, in some of the earlier Vedic hymns, this title is applied, as a mark of respect, to Indra and other beneficent deities.[3] But, in later passages, the Asuras appear in quite a different light. It would seem that, after the rupture between the Devas and Ahuras, the latter term, or its equivalent Asura, was applied by the Devas to enemies in general; just as Deva, or Daeva, became

[1] Atharva Veda, viii. 3, 3.
[2] Essays on the Parsi Religion, 268, 269.
[3] Rig Veda, I. xxiv. 14; IV. ii. 5.

a term of reproach in Iran. Hence the hostile serpent tribes became Asuras.

These people were enemies, both of the Ahuras and of the Devas, from a very early period ; even before the separation of these two branches of the Aryan family.

We learn, from the Vendidad, that the appearance of a mighty serpent, created by Angra Mainyu, was one cause of the migration from Airyāna Vāejo.[1] Whether this mighty serpent was the Azi-dahāka, who overthrew and killed Yima,[2] is uncertain. Both, however, doubtless belonged to the same race, as did probably "the horse-devouring, man-devouring, serpent Sruara," which at a later period was killed by the Iranian hero Keresaspa.[3]

The title Azi-dahāka (the devouring serpent) which was given to the destroyer of Yima, was held afterwards by a long succession of rulers. This dynasty is said to have lasted for a thousand years,[4] and to have ended with Bevārāsp. This king, who is described as having been overthrown by Feridūn, and as having been condemned to be bound to the mountain of Demāvand,[5] has been identified with Astyages, who, according to Herodotus, was overthrown by Cyrus.[6]

[1] Vendidad, Fargard I. [2] Bundahis, xxxi. 5. Zamyad Yast, 46.
[3] Zamyad Yast, 40. [4] Bundahis, xxxiv. 5.
[5] Ib. xxix. 9. [6] Herodotus, Clio, cxxviii.

Astyages was apparently the same as Istuvegu, who is described by Nabonidos, King of Babylon, and by Cyrus, as having been defeated by the latter at Ekbatana or Agamtanu.[1]

This identification of Azi-dahāka with Istuvegu is not quite certain, but the account given of the latter in the cuneiform inscriptions agrees in so many respects with the descriptions recorded of Astyages by Herodotus, and of Azi-dahāka or Bevārāsp, in the Bundehis, that the same chief seems to be referred to in each case.

Moreover, Azi-dahāka was evidently a dynastic title; Bevārāsp was also a title; while Istuvegu appears to have been the name of the king to whom these titles were applied.

Astyages has been considered as a Median ruler, and was so described by Herodotus,[2] but, according to inscriptions of Nabonidos, King of Babylon, he was chief of the "Tsab Manda," or Barbarian host.[3] This may, however, have been merely a derisive epithet.

Astyages and his predecessors were powerful rivals of the Babylonian kings. Kastarit or Cyaxares, father of Astyages, with other chiefs, overthrew Assyria.[4] And one of the prede-

[1] "Records of Past," N.S., v. 159.

[2] Herodotus, Thalia, lxii., Clio, xcvi.

[3] "Ancient Empires of East," 241.

[4] Ib. 141, 240.

cessors of Istuvegu appears to have invaded Babylonia.

An astronomical tablet of early date records: "The Tsab Manda comes and governs the land. The altars of the great gods are taken away. Bel goes to the land of Elam."[1]

Media and Elam bordered upon Ellipi, which was the chief seat of the power of Astyages,[2] and Media was doubtless included in his dominions. His royal city was Ekbatana, or Agamtanu, now Hamadan,[3] which was built by his ancestor Deiokes, who appears to have united the different tribes of Media under his rule.[4]

Inscriptions of Nabonidos and Cyrus say that Istuvegu was defeated by the latter. These records, however, agree with the account given in the Bundehis, that the invader was aided by an insurrection. They also mention that Istuvegu was delivered up to the conqueror by his own army.[5]

It seems not unlikely that one cause of this revolt was, as suggested by Firdūsi,[6] the religious zeal of the king, and his encouragement of the cruel rites and human sacrifices connected with

[1] "Records of Past," N.S., Pref., I. xiv. [2] Ib. v. 153.

[3] "Ancient Empires of East," 240.

[4] Herodotus, Clio, xcviii., c.; "Ancient Empires of East," 239. [5] "Records of Past," N.S., v. 159.

[6] Shahnama, Atkinson, 41.

serpent-worship. Or it may be that, like Jemshid or Yima,[1] and other Solar kings to be referred to later, Istuvegu himself claimed divine honours, as an incarnation of the Sun-god, and that the serpents, said to have grown from his shoulders, were those forming the canopy over the head of his sculptured representation in his temple. Herodotus tells us that the king himself was never seen in public.[2]

According to the Shāhnama, the serpents attending upon Zahāk, or Azi-dahāka, required to be fed daily with the brains of human victims. And the blacksmith Gāvah, when it fell to the lot of his two sons to be sacrificed, raised an insurrection, of which Feridūn took advantage.[3] The leather apron of Gāvah, which was used by the rebels as a banner, became afterwards the sacred standard of Persia, and continued to be so, until the Mohammedan conquest of that country, many centuries later.

From the above it seems that the kings of Media and other neighbouring countries, down to the time of Astyages, were serpent-worshippers, and were known by the dynastic title of Azi-dahāka. They doubtless all belonged to the same race, if not to the same tribe, as that Azi-dahāka who "sawed Yima in twain."[4]

[1] Mirkhond, Shea, 116.
[2] Herodotus, Clio, xcix.
[3] Shahnama, Atkinson, 41.
[4] Zamyad Yast, 73.

Ahi and Azi both mean serpent, and both were tribal or dynastic titles—not personal names. The epithet dahāka is not applied to Ahi in the Rig Veda, nor is it there said that Vritra was the destroyer of Yima, who was the Yama of the Hindus.[1] It seems, however, tolerably certain that the Ahi of the Rig Veda and the Azi of the Zend Avesta, represent chiefs of the same widely-spread Sun-worshipping people, whose emblem was the many-headed serpent. There can also be little doubt that "the Turanian Dānus of victorious strength," described in the Zend Avesta,[2] were the same people as the Dānavas, or sons of Dānu, of the Rig Veda and the Mahābhārata. Of these, as we have already seen, Vritra, the Ahi, was one of the most powerful chiefs.

Azi of the Zend Avesta is said to have had three heads and six eyes.[3] In the Rig Veda the same description is applied to Asura chiefs. Thus we find: "Thou, Lord (Indra), humbled and subjugated the loud-shouting Dasa, with six eyes and three heads.[4]

We learn too from the Satapatha Brāhmana, that Twashtri had a son called Visvarupa, who

[1] "Relig. of Parsis," Haug, 277.

[2] Aban Yast., 73; Favardin Yast, 37, 38.

[3] Aban Yast., 34; Zamyad Yast, 37.

[4] Rig Veda, X. xcix. 6.

had three heads and six eyes, and was killed by Indra.[1] This son of Twashtri is called, in the Mahābhārata, the great Asura.[2]

In each of these instances the hoods of the protecting serpents, expanded over the head of the Nāga raja, are no doubt referred to.

The passage just quoted from the Rig Veda is of great importance, as it shows that the three-headed Nāga, of the epic poems, was known to the Vedic rishis, and was not an invention of later times.

Zahāk, or Azi-dahāka, as already mentioned, is said to have had serpents growing from his shoulders. Some of the sculptured representations of the Nāga demigods in India have this appearance; but, in most cases, the tail of the serpent is shown at the back of the figure, over the head of which its hoods are spread out.

Vritra and Arbuda have been shown to have been Asuras, Dānavas, and serpent chiefs. It seems to follow, therefore, that Namuchi, Urana, Sushna, Sambara, Pipru, and other Daityas and Dānavas, whose struggles with Indra, or his followers, are the subject of so many of the Vedic hymns, were also chiefs of tribes who opposed the Āryas, and not drought, or climatic in-

[1] Satapatha Br., I. ii. 3, 2.

[2] Mahābhārata, Udyoga, Sainyodyoga, p. xvi.

BĀSDEO (VĀSUKI),
BIJEH,
CHINĀB VALLEY.

fluences personified, as supposed by the commentator Sayana.

This writer, living long after the events described in the hymns, and far distant from the scene of their occurrence, was evidently misled by the figurative language of the Vedic rishis. Modern scholars, however, seem to be less and less inclined to rely upon the Brahman commentators.[1]

The following passages from the Rig Veda, taken in connexion with those already quoted, seem to show clearly that the conflicts with the Asuras were real battles. In many of these Indra fought, or was believed to have fought, in defence of rishis or rajas, who were his worshippers. Thus in one hymn we find: "Thou (Indra) didst hurl down the Dāsa Sambara from the mountain, thou didst preserve Divodāsa."[2] And again: "Thou didst cast down the Dāsa Sambara, son of Kulitara, from the great mountain."[3] Further we have: "Munificent hero, who easily conquerest thy foes, thou didst put to flight the Dasyus in battle."[4] Then we have the prayer: "Discriminate between the Āryas and they who are Dasyus, restraining those who perform no religious rites; compel

[1] Rhys Davids, "Budd. Ind.," 152.
[2] Rig Veda, VI. xxvi. 5; Muir, ii. 384.
[3] Ib. IV. xxx. 14; Muir, ii. 380. [4] Rig Veda, I. lxiii. 4.

them to submit to the performer of sacrifices."[1] This evidently referred to men and not to clouds. We are told too that "Indra shattered, for Divodāsa, the hundred castles of Sambara."[2] And again we find: "Indra, wielder of the thunderbolt, warring on behalf of Pūrukutsa, thou didst overthrow the seven cities; thou didst cut off, for Sudās, the wealth of Anhas."[3] In another hymn we have: "Benevolent to man, thou hast broken the cities of Pipru; and protected Rijisvān in his battles with the Dasyus."[4] Further, we find: "Thou didst boldly sweep away the wealth of Sushna; thou didst shatter his castles."[5] In another place it is said: "Indra, in his might, quickly demolished all their strongholds and their seven cities. He has given the dwelling of the son of Anu to Tritsu; may we (by propitiating Indra) conquer in battle the ill-speaking man."[6]

From the passages just quoted it seems evident that the Asuras and Dasyus were neither demons nor climatic phenomena, but chiefs of tribes who were hostile to the Āryas, as indeed they were represented to be, in the epic poems.

Taking into consideration the whole of the foregoing evidence, it appears impossible to arrive

[1] Rig Veda, I. li. 8.
[2] Ib. II. xix. 6.
[3] Ib. I. lxiii. 7.
[4] Ib. I. li. 5.
[5] Rig Ved., IV. xxx. 13.
[6] Rig Ved., VII. xviii. 13.

at any other conclusion than that the Nāgas of the epic poems were the Asuras, Dasyus, Daityas, Dānavas, and Serpas, of the Rig Veda. And it seems scarcely less certain that the serpent-worshipping people, to whom these epithets were applied, were of the same race as the tribes represented by the Azi and the sons of Dānu, of the Zend Avesta.

The rugged country of Afghanistan was probably the scene of most of the conflicts with the Ahi. Indeed the mountains, so frequently alluded to in the Rig Veda, could only have been met with before the Āryas or Devas crossed the Indus.

We shall see later that Kābulistan was ruled by serpent chiefs in the early days of the Persian empire; that the rulers of the neighbouring state of Ghor, down to the time of the Mohammedan invasion, claimed descent from the same race; and that, until the conversion of the people to the faith of Islām, the Nāga demigods were the popular deities everywhere between Kābul and the Indus.

We learn from the Satapatha Brāhmana that Vritra was a serpent and a Dānava.[1]

We learn too from the Mahābhārata, that tribes of fierce Dānavas, who were invincible in battle, and were known as Kālakeyas, were

[1] Satapatha Brahmana, S.B.E., 1, 6, 3, 9.

under the lordship of Vritra. And that this "prince of the Daityas" was then "occupying the whole earth and the heavens."[1] Apparently, therefore, Vritra claimed paramount power, and probably also divine honours, as did so many Solar chiefs.

The Kālakeyas, who were also called Kāleyas or Kālakhanjas, sprang from Vishnu, or the Sun; and they lived in the territory of Pātala,[2] that is, in the Indus valley and neighbouring country. Nāga rajas appear to have succeeded Vritra, the great Ahi, in this portion of his dominions.

We have it, on the authority of the Mahābhārata, that the great Asura Arbuda was a Nāga raja.[3] And, from the genealogy of the Solar race, we learn that the name of one of the royal family of Ajudhia was Ahi Nāga.[4] We find too that Ahi Deva was a demigod worshipped in Kashmir.[5]

The chief deity of the Asuras, as we have seen in the case of the Kāleyas, was the Sun, or rather perhaps the Sun-god, from whom they believed themselves to be descended. They also venerated the Nāga, or hooded-serpent, as the protector

[1] Mahābhārata, Vana, Tirthayatra, pp. c., ci.
[2] Ib., Udyoga, Bhagavatyana, p. xcix.
[3] Ib., Sabha, Jarasandha-badha, p. xxi.
[4] Vishnu Purana, Wilson, IV. iv. 386.
[5] Rajatarangini, Dutt, 176.

BĀSDEO (VĀSUKI),
CHAMBA.

or totem of their race. The hood of one or more of these serpents, expanded over his head, was the distinctive mark of a Nāga demigod, or deified Solar chief.

Sūrya, the Hindu Sun-god, is represented with a canopy over his head, formed of the hoods of a seven-headed Nāga;[1] so also is the Asura Rāhu, and so too are the Nāga demigods Vāsuki or Bāska Nāga, Indru Nāga, and other serpent deities. This is strong evidence of the identity of the Asuras, or Nāgas, with the Indian branch of the Solar race, but further proof will not be wanting.

The term Nāga does not appear to have been a tribal name, but merely an appellation used, by Brahmanical writers, to distinguish those who venerated the Nāga, or hooded-serpent.

There can be no doubt that this serpent was held sacred by all the Asuras, as it was by other people who claimed Solar descent.

So generally, throughout the world, was the Nāga held sacred, that it would seem to have been the earliest totem of the wide-spread Solar race. It appears to have been adopted before the occurrence of that subdivision into tribes, which apparently gave rise to the great number of totems of later times.

We find that amongst the Asuras or Nāgas

[1] Elliot, "Races of the N.W. Provinces," i. 75.

were included various tribes, and that these were distinguished by different totems, or sub-totems. But the Nāg was common to all, and the Sun was worshipped by all.

According to some Brahmanical authorities, both Asuras and Āryas were children of Kāsyapa, though by different wives.[1]

This progenitor of the Solar race is identified with the Sun and with the tortoise.[2] It is probable that he was either the Sun-god, or a very early deified Solar chief.

We learn from the Satapatha Brāhmana that: "This tortoise (Kāsyapa) is the same as yonder sun."[3]

The tortoise was one of the earliest and most widely spread totems of the Solar race.

The various birds, beasts, reptiles, and other objects, assigned as progeny to Kāsyapa, doubtless represent the totems, or sub-totems, of different Solar tribes.

Kāsyapa has been connected, and apparently with good reason, with the Kaspian sea, and the tribes living to the south of it.[4]

The rishi Vrihaspati went to the "Sea of Milk" to consult "the great Kāsyapa."[5] The

[1] Mahābhārata, Adi, Sambhava, p. lxiv.

[2] Atharva Veda, xiii. 3, 10; xix. 53, 10.

[3] Satapatha Brāhmana, vii. v. 1, 5, 6 (S.B.E.).

[4] "Iran und Turan," 51. [5] Harivansa, Langlois, II. 28.

Sea of Milk, which surrounded Sāka dwipa,[1] or the Scythian country, has been identified with the Kaspian.[2]

There are frequent references, in the Vedic hymns, to the withholding of rain by the Asuras, and especially by the great chief Vritra, and to the consequent drought ceasing on the death of the enemy. These passages relate to the belief, which survives to this day, that the Nāga rajas were able to control the elements. One of the Vedic hymns, describing a conflict between Indra and Ahi, or Vritra, thus refers to this power: "Neither the lightning, nor the thunder (discharged by Vritra), nor the rain which he showered, nor the thunderbolt, harmed Indra when he and Ahi contended.[3]

Believing the Asura chiefs to have this power over the elements, it was only natural that the worshippers of Indra should apply to him for protection, when suffering from drought or tempest caused, as they supposed, by the influence of their enemies.

The folklore of northern India is full of legends connected with this power of the Nāgas. These demigods are still propitiated, before any other deity, when the country is suffering from drought

[1] Vishnu Purāna, Wilson, II. iv. 200.
[2] "Iran und Turan," 7.
[3] Rig Veda, I. xxxii. 13.

or excessive rain. And tradition says that human sacrifices were common, on such occasions, in days gone by.

Buddhist writers make frequent allusions to the command over the elements exercised by the Nāgas. Thus we learn from the Mahāwanso, that when, in the time of Asoka, the thero Majjhantiko was sent to Kashmir and Gandhāra, to convert the people to the religion of Buddha, the Nāga raja Aravalo, to terrify him, caused a violent storm, with rain, thunder, lightning, and thunderbolts. The thero, however, was unmoved, and the raja became a convert.[1]

The Chinese Buddhist pilgrims frequently allude to this power of the Nāgas or Dragons. Sung-Yun says that Buddha travelled to Udyāna to convert a Nāga king, who, being angry, caused a violent storm with rain.[2]

Fah-Hian tells how, in his time (400 A.D.), the dragons of the Tsung-ling mountains caused wind, rain, snow, etc.[3]

The same pilgrim says that the friendly dragon at Sankisa caused fertilizing rain, and that Buddhist priests conducted the worship at his temple.[4]

In the seventh century Hiouen-Tsiang found

[1] Mahawanso, Turnour, xii. 72.

[2] "Buddhist Records of W. World," I. xcv.

[3] Ib. I. xxix.

[4] Ib. I. xli.

the people of Takshasilā going in procession, with Sramanas, to pray for rain at the shrine of Elapatra Nāga.[1]

To this day the rulers of the Hindu Kush states Hunza and Nagar, though now Mohammedans, are believed, by their subjects, to be able to command the elements.[2]

This power is still ascribed to the serpent-gods in the Sun-worshipping countries of China, Manchuria, and Korea, and was so, until the introduction of Christianity, in Mexico and Peru.

This supposed ability of the Nāga rajas to control the elements, and especially the waters, arising no doubt from their connexion with the Sun, led apparently to their association with springs, streams, and lakes. In these the serpent deities were supposed to dwell, although the Cobra is not a water-snake, and cannot live under water.

Every lake and every spring in Kashmir, and in many other parts of India, was sacred to one or other of the Nāga demigods, or to the sun.

Near most temples of the sun is to be seen a pool, or tank, of clear water. This is called "Şūraj Kund," or pool of the sun, and is sacred to the Sun-god. Many legends tell of the terrible storms and other disasters which have followed any defilement of the sacred waters. A pool or

[1] "Buddhist Records of W. World," i. 137.
[2] "Tribes of Hindu Kush," Biddulph, 95.

spring is also to be found at many of the Nāga temples.

The sun and the serpent appear to have been everywhere connected with the sea, rivers, and lakes, and, in fact, with the waters generally.

In India, Vishnu, who is a form of the Sun-god,[1] is represented as floating upon the ocean, supported by the many-headed serpent.

The great temple of Mārtānda in Kashmir was built at a tirtha, or sacred spring, which was dedicated to the Sun-god, as Mārtānda, or Vishnu-Sūrya.[2]

[1] Macdonell (Myth. Studies in R.V.), J.R.A.S., 1895, p. 175.

[2] Rajatarangini, Stein, iv. 192.

RUINED TEMPLE OF THE SUN-GOD AT MĀRTAND, KASHMIR.

CHAPTER II

THE Asuras, Dasyus, or Nāgas, with whom the Āryas came into contact, on approaching the borders of India, were no savage aboriginal tribes, but a civilized people who had cities and castles. Some of these are said, in the Veda, to have been built of stone.

It would seem, indeed, as if the Asuras had reached a higher degree of civilisation than their Āryan rivals. Some of their cities were, as we shall soon see, places of considerable importance. And, in addition to this, wealth and luxury, the use of magic, superior architectural skill, and ability to restore the dead to life, were ascribed to the Asuras by Brahmanical writers.

It is probable that part of the magic was superior mechanical skill. The secret of the process by which their enemies were brought back to life, which was long sought in vain by the Āryas,[1] was most likely a knowledge of surgery, and of the use of medicines. By this means, the sick and wounded may have been restored to life, if not the dead.

We learn further, also on Brahmanical authority,

[1] Mahābhārata, Adi, Sambhava, p. lxxvi.

that the ancient sage Garga, one of the fathers of Indian astronomy, having propitiated Sesha Nāga, acquired from him a knowledge of astronomical science, of the planets, and of the good and evil denoted by the aspect of the heavens.[1]

The Nāgas occupy a very prominent position in connexion with Indian astronomy, and this is not likely to have been assigned to them, by their Brahmanical rivals, without good reason. Probably this and other branches of science were brought, by the Asuras, from their ancient home in the countries between the Kaspian and the Persian Gulf.

The close relationship between the Indian and the Chaldean astronomical systems has been frequently noticed.

The sun-worship of the Asuras; their holding sacred the Nāga or hooded serpent, sometimes represented with many heads; their deification of kings and of ancestors; their veneration for the cedar; their religious dances; their sacrificial rites; their communication with the deities, through the medium of inspired prophets; their occasional tendency towards democratic institutions; their use of tribal emblems or totems; and many of their social customs; seem to connect them with that very early civilization—Turanian or otherwise—which we find amongst so many of

[1] Vishnu Purāna, II. v. 206.

TEMPLE OF KÂRSHA NĀG, SUILL VALLEY.

the peoples of extreme antiquity. They had, in fact, much in common with the early inhabitants of Babylonia; and, perhaps, even more with those of Elam and the neighbouring countries.

We shall see, later, that the Asuras and the Dravidians were, apparently, the same people.

Of the cities described as belonging to the Asuras, Pātala, Prāgjyotisha, Saubha, Hiranyapura and Takshasilā were all places of wealth and importance, on or near the Indus. Magadha, Matharā and other cities in the valley of the Ganges seem also to have been established by the Asuras, at a very early period. Visālāpura, or Ujaini, too, appears to have been a Nāga city, as we shall presently see.

We find Krishna pointing out to Arjuna, in the neighbourhood of Magadha, the places where dwelt, "of old," those Nāgas Arbuda and Chakravapin, "those persecutors of all enemies"; also "the Nāga Swastika and that other excellent Nāga called Mani."[1] The tirtha of Mani Nāga is mentioned in the Mahābhārata as a sacred place of pilgrimage, which was widely known even at that early period.[2] Like other holy places of the Asuras, it was taken over by their Brahmanical successors.

Matharā, or Madarā, is said to have been founded

[1] Mahābhārata, Sabhā, Jarasandhabadha, p. xxi.
[2] Ib., Vana, Tirthayatra, p. lxxiv.

by the Asura Madhu; from whose son, Lavana, it was taken by Satrughna, brother of Rāma.[1]

Pātala was the capital of the territory which bore the same name, and which, as already noticed, appears to have been included in the dominions of Vritra, the great Ahi.

In Pātala reigned the royal rishi Kapila Vāsudeva, or Kapila Nāga, who destroyed the sons of Sagara.[2] Ikshvāku, too, from whom so many Solar dynasties claim descent, was a raja of Pātala.[3]

As Sakya Buddha was of Solar race, and a descendant of Ikshvāku, Buddhist authorities were much interested in these dynasties. From this source we learn that nineteen capital cities were founded by descendants of Ikshvāku, viz. Kusawati, Ayojapura, Baranasi, Kapila, Hatthipura, Ekachakra, Wajirawati, Madhura, Aritthapura Indapatta, Kosambi, Kanagochi, Roja, Champa, Mithila, Rajagaha, Takkasilā, Kusinara, and Tamalitti.[4] All these were important cities, and the capitals of considerable states.

From Pātala, and neighbouring ports, the

[1] Vishnu Purāna, IV. iv. 385.

[2] Mahābhārata, Udyoga, Bhagavatyana, p. cviii. Vishnu Purāna, IV. iv. 378.

[3] Mahawanso, Turnour, Intro. xxxv.; Rockhill (Dulva) 11; Rajavali, Upham, ii. 159.

[4] Mahawanso, Intro. xxxv.

Asuras or Nāgas sent out expeditions to raid, or to colonize, the neighbouring coasts. Here, too, in later times, Alexander fitted out his fleet.

Saubha, also a city of the Asuras, was taken by Krishna ; and its ruler Salwa, son of a Daitya, was killed near the seashore.[1]

Pragjyotisha, called " the great and impregnable city of the Asuras," was captured, and its ruler, Naraka, slain by the same Yadava hero.[2] The city seems, however, to have regained its independence, as Bhāgadatta, one of its later chiefs, is said to have ruled the west like another Varuna.[3] This appears to mean that he claimed the sovereignty of the sea.

Hiranyapura, the city of the great Asura Hiranyakasipu, and the scene of the man-lion avatar, was, according to tradition, the present Multān. The great temple of the Sun, at this city, was celebrated throughout India from the earliest period to the time of the Moslem invaders.

Takshasilā, the Taxila of the Greeks, was the chief city of the Nāga people in the north of India. According to the Vayu Purāna, this city was founded by Taksha, son of Bhārata the brother of Rāma, of the Solar race.[4] It was, as we have just

[1] Mahābhārata, Vana, Arjuna-bhigamana, p. xxii.
[2] Mahābhārata, Udyoga, Yanasandhi, p. xlvii.
[3] Ib., Sabhā, Rajasuyarambha, p. xiv.
[4] Vishnu Purāna (Halls ed.), IV. iv. 219.

seen, the capital of one of the Solar kingdoms, founded by the race of Ikshvāku, and it was the city of Takshaka Nāga. This is still further proof that the Solar dynasties, descended from Ikshvāku, were of Asura or Nāga origin.

It was on his return from a raid into the country of Takshasilā that Janamejaya, the Bhārāta raja of Indraprastha, at the instigation of the Brāhman Utanka, held his serpent sacrifice.[1] The victims, on this occasion, were the Nāga prisoners taken in the raid, who were burned alive, with Brahmanical rites, as recorded in the Mahābhārata.[2]

The legend of the serpent-sacrifice is known all over India. In the Panjāb, it is one of the most popular folk-tales. Tradition says that, in consequence of the abduction of a daughter of Bāsak Nāg, by the raja Parikshit, Indraprastha was invaded by a Nāga army and Parikshit was killed. His son, Janamejaya, afterwards carried on an exterminating war with the Nāgas, which resulted in the serpent-sacrifice.

Not only were the Asuras or Nāgas a civilized people, but they were a maritime power. Holding both banks of the great river Indus, they must have had access to the sea from a very early period. Their kinship, too, with the serpent-worshipping

[1] Mahābhārata, Adi, Pausya, p. iii.
[2] Ib., Adi, Astika, p. lii.

TEMPLE OF BÂSDEO (VĀSUKI),
BIJEH, CHINĀB VALLEY.

people of ancient Media, and the neighbouring countries, which has already been referred to, must have led to a very early development of trade with the Persian Gulf.

The Asuras were actively engaged in "The Churning of the Ocean,"[1] which is but an allegorical description of sea-borne commerce in its early days.

It is probable that the Mandara mountain, said to have been used in the churning process, represented a ship, described in the florid and exaggerated manner of Oriental poets.

The chariot of Varuna, the sea-god, is represented as having been drawn by three-headed Nāgas.[2]

Before the Āryas, or Devas, could engage in the "Churning of the Ocean," they were obliged to apply for the help of the Asuras.[3] Then we find that Hari (Vishnu) told the Devas that, in order to obtain the assistance of the Daityas, in "churning the ocean," they must be at peace with them, and promise to give them an equal share of the produce.[4] At a later period than that here referred to, in the time of Manu, both Devas and Nāgas probably engaged in commerce, and laws

[1] Mahābhārata, Adi, Astika, p. xviii.
[2] Harivansa, Langlois, II. 421.
[3] Mahābhārata, Adi, Astika, p. xviii.
[4] Vishnu Purāna, I. ix. 75.

were made for its regulation.[1] But then the relations between Āryas and Dasyus had become greatly modified, and the union between the two peoples had made considerable progress.

The ships mentioned in the Rig Veda, in connexion with the Aswins,[2] probably belonged to the Asuras. The Āryas, at that time, could have had no access to the sea, unless through the country of their enemies.

In the Mahābhārata, the ocean is described as the habitation of the Nāgas and the residence of the Asuras ; it is also said to be the refuge of the defeated Asuras.[3] This was no doubt because marauding bands of this people retreated to their ships after an unsuccessful raid. Thus we find that, on the death of Vritra, his followers took refuge in the sea.[4] So also did the Asura Panchajāna, who lived in Pātala, when he was pursued by Krishna.[5] And so did the Dānavas when defeated by the Devas at the churning of the ocean.[6]

An ancient legend, given in the Mahābhārata, relates how Kadru, mother of the serpents, compelled Garuda to convey her sons across the sea " to a beautiful country, in a distant region, which

[1] Manu, Haughton, i. 83, 5 ; Ib. i. 33, 15.
[2] Rig Veda, I. xxxiii. 15.
[3] Mahābhārata, Adi, Astika, p. xxii.
[4] Mahābhārata, Vana, Tirthayatra, p. ciii.
[5] Vishnu Purāna, V. xxi. 526.
[6] Mahābhārata, Adi, Astika, p. xix.

was inhabited by Nāgas." After encountering a violent storm and great heat, the sons of Kadru were landed in the country of Ramāniaka, on the Malabar coast.

This territory had been occupied previously by a fierce Asura named Lavana.[1] So there had been a still earlier colonization by the same race.

Nāga chiefs are frequently mentioned as ruling countries in or under the sea. Thus Yādu the son of Hariāswa, who was a son of Ikshvāku, was carried off by the Nāga raja Dhūmavarna, whose kingdom was beneath the sea. This kingdom was called Ratna-dwipa (the land of gems), and the people there had ships and trade, and fished for pearls.

Yādu married the five daughters of the Nāga chief; and Harita, one of his sons, succeeded his grandfather in this island kingdom, which was perhaps Ceylon.[2]

Rāvana, the great raja of Lanka, or Ceylon, on one of his marauding expeditions, was attacked by Indra and his followers. Rāvana's army took to flight, but was rallied by Meghanada, who took Indra prisoner and carried him off to Lanka.[3]

In this instance, as in others in which the deities are represented as leading their followers in battle,

[1] Mahābhārata, Adi, Astika, p. xxvii.

[2] Harivansa, i. 399, 401.

[3] Rāmāyana, Yaddha kanda, O.S.T., iv. 495.

it is probable that the inspired prophet, carrying the image or standard of the god at the head of the army, is alluded to, and not Indra in person. These prophets will be referred to later.

We find that, on another occasion, Rāvana invaded the dominions of Arjuna Kartavirya, on the banks of the Narbada, and was himself taken prisoner.[1] In each case the invader could only have arrived by sea; and he must have had considerable naval resources to enable him to do so.

Raids, such as these, appear to have been frequent upon the coasts of India; and probably similar descents were made upon the shores of neighbouring countries.

Rāvana, though called in the Rāmāyana a Rakshas, was an Asura, and he was doubtless the ruler of one of the Nāga colonies. We find that his grandfather and other members of his family lived in Pātala.[2] His great-uncle, Virupaksha, called in the Mahābhārata the great Asura,[3] was a son of Dānu.[4] The identity of the Asuras and the Dravidians has already been referred to.

Virupaksha, who is mentioned in the Grihya Sutras as a divine being entitled to worship,[5] was, according to Buddhist authorities, chief of serpents

[1] Vishnu Purāna, IV. xi. 417.

[2] Rāmāyana, Uttara K., Muir, iv. 486.

[3] Mahābhārata, Adi, Sambhava, p. lxvii. [4] Ib. p. lxv.

[5] Sankhayana Grihya Sutras, 14, 18, 1.

SHRINE OF DĀNU DEO,
RĀMGURH, KAMAON.

and regent of the west. Buddha himself says that the Virupakshas are a royal race of serpents.[1]

The ten heads ascribed to Rāvana were, no doubt, those of the protecting serpents forming the canopy over his head, as a Nāga raja. Indrajit, son of Rāvana, bore the device of a golden serpent upon his banner, and Usanas, the chief priest of the Asuras, or more probably one of his descendants, officiated at his sacrifices.[2]

From the foregoing, it seems evident that at a very early period, even before any alliance with the Āryas, the Asuras were expert navigators, possessed very considerable naval resources, and had founded colonies upon distant coasts.

The trident of Neptune was borrowed from the Nāga demigods, and the conch-shell of the Tritons was used by the Asuras before them.

The connexion of the Nāgas with the ocean, and with countries beyond it, might seem to indicate that they found their way to India by sea. But their very early occupation of northern India, and of the slopes of the Hindu Kush and Himālaya, is against this; as is also their connexion with the serpent tribes of Kābulistan and further west, which has been mentioned and will be again referred to. As already noted, however, the Asuras were akin to some of the peoples bordering upon the Persian

[1] Chullavagga, v. 6, 1; Jatakas, Fausboll, ii. 145, P. T. Soy., 1888. [2] Rāmāyana, Uttara K., Muir, iv. 416.

Gulf, and, with these, communication was doubtless kept up by sea.

Up to the end of the Vedic period, warfare between Āryas and Dasyus continued with varying results. The Asuras appear to have been engaged in many intertribal conflicts ; and the Āryas seem to have allied themselves sometimes with one tribe and sometimes with another. We find, too, that the rishis, and other religious ascetics, went backwards and forwards, between Devas and Asuras, and were equally well received by both.[1] The rishi Nārada is said to have known all the inhabitants of Pātala, and he had evidently a very high opinion of them.[2] As time went on, commercial arrangements were entered into, such as those alluded to in the legend of " The Churning of the Ocean."

At a very early period, too, intermarriages seem to have taken place, even in the highest quarters. Sachi, the wife of Indra, was the daughter of the Asura chief Puloman ;[3] and Jayanti, Indra's daughter, became the wife of Usanas, the chief priest of the Asuras.[4] Then Mātali, the " friend, counsellor, and charioteer " of Indra, married his

[1] Vishnu Purāna, II. v. 204.

[2] Mahābhārata, Udyoga, Bhagavatyana, p. xcvii.

[3] Rāmāyana, Yuddha K., Muir, II. 405.

[4] Bhāgavata Purāna, Muir, v. 154.

daughter, Gunakesi, to the Nāga Sumukha, of the race of Airāvata.[1]

Many others, both Brāhmans and Kshtriyas, followed these examples, and intermarried with the Asuras. The Mahābhārata abounds with instances of this.

Somasrava, who was the family priest of the Pandava raja Janamejaya,[2] and the Brāhman Astika, whose influence put a stop to the serpent-sacrifice of that monarch,[3] were both sons of Nāga mothers. And the Nāga chief Āryaka was grandfather of Sura, king of the Surasenas, who was father of Kunti, wife of Pandu, and of Vasudeva, father of Krishna.[4]

This shows that the family connexions between Āryas and Asuras had become intimate.

Under such circumstances as these, it seems only natural that the enmity between the two races should have become less bitter, and that the demons of the Rig Veda should, at a later period, have assumed a different complexion. This we find was actually the case.

Thus, Arbuda, the Asura warrior of the Rig Veda, and the son of Kadru, is called in the Aitareya Brāhmana, " the serpent rishi, framer of

[1] Mahābhārata, Udyoga, Bhagavatyāna, p. ciii.
[2] Ib., Adi, Pausya, p. iii.
[3] Ib., Adi, Astika, p. liv.
[4] Ib., Adi, Sambhava, p. cxxviii.

mantras" ;[1] and Indra is said, in the Sāma Veda, to have drunk the Soma of Kadrū, mother of the serpents, in the full assembly.[2]

In fact, the fusion which occurred between the Āryas and the Dasyus, in India, greatly resembled the union which took place, in Babylonia, between the Semite and the Accadian peoples.

In the Atharva Veda, Takshaka Vaisālya, Irāvan, and Dhritarashtra, who are all Nāga demi-gods, are mentioned by name as divine beings.[3]

In the Grihya Sutras, the serpents—no longer enemies—are invoked as deities: "To the divine hosts of the serpents Swaha!" It should be noted, too, that the serpents are here called Nāgas.[4]

Takshaka Vaisālya again, and Virupaksha, who is also a serpent demi-god, are said, in the Grihya Sutras, to be entitled to oblations with the formula Swaha![5]

According to the Paraskara Grihya Sutra, oblations are to be offered to "The lord of the overpowering serpents belonging to Sūrya."[6] This fully confirms what has been said as to the connexion between the sun and the serpent.

The passages just cited show that, in the course

[1] Aitareya Brāhmana, VI. i. 1 (Haug).
[2] Sāma Veda, II. iv. 7.
[3] Atharva Veda, VIII. ix. 2.
[4] Asvalāyana Grihya Sutra, II. i. 91; III. iv. 1.
[5] Sankhyana Grihya Sutra, xiv. 18, 1.
[6] Paraskara Grihya Sutra, ii. 14, 9.

TEMPLE OF SABIR NĀG,
CHINTA,
CHINĀB VALLEY.

of time, very great changes had taken place in the religion and sentiment of the Āryas; and that great progress had been made towards the union of the Devas and Asuras.

Although wars were still frequent between rival chiefs and hostile tribes, the gradual fusion between the two peoples continued. We find that, at the period described in the epic poems, not only had the religion and mode of life, as represented in the Rig Veda, undergone great modifications, but the distinction between Ārya and Dasyu, or Deva and Asura, had almost disappeared. All had become Kshatriyas. And, although even then some were more orthodox than others, all when they died went to Indra's heaven. Swarga was, in fact, shared equally by Devas and by Nāgas, and on equal terms.

Takshaka was then the friend of Indra,[1] and the friend and benefactor of the Devas.[2] This Nāga chief was dwelling with Indra, in Swarga, at the time of the serpent-sacrifice.[3]

We find, too, that, while the union of the two races was in progress, Swarga was tenanted by both Devas and Nāgas; but when the Asuras became recognized as Kshatriyas their souls became Devas.

The Devas were, and still are, the souls of de-

[1] Mahābhārata, Adi, Khandavadaha, p. ccxxxv.

[2] Ib., Adi, Astika, p. xxxix. 120.

[3] Ib., Adi, Astika, p. liii.

parted Kshatriyas, and they live with Indra in Swarga. This term is, however, applied figuratively, in the epic poems, to the living worshippers of Indra—the Āryas and the Āryanized tribes—to distinguish them from the unregenerate Asuras.

This, however, was merely a poetical use of the term, as the Devas of Swarga, who are compared with the Pitris,[1] were the souls of the warrior caste.[2] When a Rājput dies, it is commonly said that he has become a Deo or Deva. This is not said of any other caste.

In addition to the influences, tending to a union between the Devas and the Asuras, which have already been referred to, we find that Sakra the chief priest of the Asuras divided himself, by the power of asceticism, and became the spiritual guide of both the Daityas and the Devas.[3] This would seem to indicate an association of the priesthood of the Asuras with that of the Devas or Āryas. Such an arrangement would help to explain some of the changes made in the religion of the Vedas, and would have, no doubt, a powerful influence in aid of the gradual welding together of the two peoples.

Some such alliance seems to be foreshadowed in the Rig Veda, where in a hymn to Indra by the

[1] Mahābhārata, Adi, Pauloma, p. vii.
[2] Vishnu Purāna, ed. Hall, i. 97.
[3] Mahābhārata, Adi, Sambhava, p. lxvi.

rishi Savya, son of Angiras, we find: "If Usanas should sharpen thy vigour by his own, then would thy might terrify, by its intensity, both heaven and earth." [1]

It is stated, too, that the children of Angiras intermarried with the race of Bhrigu.[2]

Usanas or Sakra, who "lighted fires, said mantras, and recited the Atharva Veda," for the success of the Asuras against Indra,[3] and restored to life the Dānavas who had been killed in battle by the Devas,[4] was the son of the great rishi Bhrigu. We find, too, that the Brāhmans who were sons of Bhārgava (Bhrigu), illustrious priests and reciters of the Sāma Veda," were the spiritual guides of the Daitya chief Hiranyakasipu.[5] We further learn that the descendants of Bhrigu, "Brāhmans, declarers of the Veda," offered a hundred Aswamedhas for Bali,[6] when this Asura chief of Pātala had overcome Indra, and had taken possession of his kingdom.

It seems evident, therefore, that Bhrigu, although regarded as a Brāhman rishi, was of Asura origin. According to the Taittiriya Upanishad,

[1] Rig Veda, Wilson, I. li. 10.

[2] Harivansa, Langlois, I. xxxii. 147.

[3] Ib., ii. 452.

[4] Mahābhārata, Adi, Sambhava, p. lxxvi.

[5] Vishnu Purāna, I. xvii. 129.

[6] Bhāgavat Purāna, xvii. 39, Muir, iv. 138

Bhrigu was a son of Varuna, the sea-god,[1] which seems to point to his having arrived by sea. This rishi is also said to have been father of the goddess Sri, or Lakshmi,[2] which probably refers to his having introduced the worship of that deity. And his son Chyavāna, who married Arushi, a daughter of Manu,[3] compelled Indra to admit the Aswins, or Dioscuri, to a share of the Soma, which means, doubtless, that he introduced the worship of these divinities. This priestly family, therefore, seems to have contributed largely to the modifications which were introduced into the Vedic religion.

The goddess Sri rose from the "deep," as did her Grecian counterpart. She was one of the results of the "Churning of the Ocean." The Aswins, too, are described as "ocean-born," and they had ships.[4] It is most likely, therefore, that all these deities were brought from beyond the sea; and probably they came from the shores of the Persian Gulf.

We have just seen that the sons of Bhrigu are said to have been reciters of the Sāma and Atharva Vedas. In the Tandya Brāhmana of the Sāma Veda, are described sacrifices, called Vratyastoma, for the consecration of those who had not, hitherto,

[1] Colebrook, ed. 1858, 45.
[2] Vishnu Purāna, I. x. 82.
[3] Mahābhārata, Adi, Sambhava, p. lxvi.
[4] Rig Veda, I. xlvi. 124; I. lxvi. 3.

lived according to the laws of orthodox Brahmanism. These people, from the description given of them, were evidently Kshatriyas; and they seem to have been Asuras in process of regeneration. They drove in war-chariots, and carried bows and lances. They did not engage in agriculture or commerce; and they spoke the same language as the orthodox, but pronounced it with difficulty.[1]

This seems to indicate that a process had been discovered for the conversion of the Asuras. And it appears evident that the blending of the Āryas and Dasyus had made considerable progress, even to the adoption of a common language.

Both Solar and Lunar lines of Kshatriyas appear to have been of Asura origin.

The Asura tribes, as we have already seen, claimed descent from the Sun. We find, however, that, "from the Sun, the Moon is born."[2] We are told, too, that at the "Churning of the Ocean" the Moon arrived, and was taken possession of by Siva,[3] who is the Indian Moon-god.

The rishi Atri is said to have been the father of the Moon.[4] This means, doubtless, that the worship of the Moon was either introduced or specially favoured by this rishi, but the words have been

[1] Weber, Hist. Ind. Lit., 67.
[2] Aitareya Br. Haug, iii. 14, 535.
[3] Mahābhārata, Adi, Astika, p. xviii.
[4] Vishnu Purāna, IV. vi. 392.

taken literally. It can scarcely be contended, however, that the Brāhman Atri, who was apparently a son of Usanas,[1] was the actual progenitor of the Moon, or of the Lunar line of Kshatriyas.

No doubt the introduction of the worship of the Moon-god led to religious strife amongst the tribes. We find traces of this in the Mahābhārata, where Atri is said to have assumed the form of Soma, or the Moon-god, and of the Sun, and to have slain the Asuras.[2]

The early history of the Lunar line of kings is obscure until the reign of Purūravas, who was overthrown by the Brāhmans for evil conduct.[3]

Ayus, son of Purūravas, married the daughter of the Asura chief Rāhu, or Swarbhanu,[4] and their son was Nahush.

This king supplanted Indra, and compelled the rishis to carry his litter. He oppressed the Devas and ill-treated the Brāhmans,[5] and then fell down from heaven and became a Nāga,[6] as his ancestors were before him. Nahush is included in the list of Nāga chiefs given in the Mahābhārata,[7] and he is said, in the Harivansa, to be one of the sons

[1] Mahābhārata, Adi, Sambhava, p. lxv.

[2] Ib., Anusasana, Anusasanika, p. cxlvii.

[3] Ib., Adi, Sambhava, p. lxxv.

[4] Ib.

[5] Ib., Vana, Tirthayatra, p. ciii.

[6] Ib., Anusasana, p. xcix.

[7] Ib., Adi Astika, p. xxxv.

RUINED TEMPLE OF INDRŪ NĀG (NAHUSH),
MANJĪR, NEAR CHAMBA
(since rebuilt).

of Kadru.[1] He is worshipped to this day as Indru Nāga.

Yayāti, son of Nahush, whose wives were Devayani, daughter of Usanas or Sakra, the Asura priest, and Sarmishta, daughter of the Daitya chief Vrishaparvan,[2] was the father of the orthodox Yadu and Puru, who were ancestors of the heroes of the Mahābhārata.

Nahush, and other kings before him, claimed divine honours. And it was doubtless as the deity, that this chief compelled the Brāhmans to carry his litter.

This union of royalty with divinity was no doubt an ancient institution, and the priestly caste seems to have acquiesced in it. But when Nahush became too overbearing, and kicked the rishi Agastya on the head, to make him go faster, his conduct was resented, and he fell down from heaven.[3] In other words, the Brāhmans raised an insurrection against him, and dethroned him.

It was probably as the Sun-god incarnate that these early kings supplanted Indra.

Prithu, and Vena before him, claimed divine honours.

According to the Harivansa, Vena defied the Brāhmans, and said, " It is to me that sacrifices

[1] Harivansa Langlois, I, 22.

[2] Mahābhārata, Adi, Sambhava, pp. lxxxi., lxxxii.

[3] Mahābhārata, Anusasana, Anusasanika, p. c.

should be presented and oblations offered. I, if I willed, could burn up the earth, or deluge it with water."[1] This king evidently claimed to have power over the elements, as the Sun-god incarnate. He seems to have been assassinated, or otherwise got rid of, by the priests.

Of his successor Prithu, who is called a Chakravarti raja, it is said that Brahmā, beholding in his hand the discus of Vishnu (the Sun), recognized in him a portion of that divinity.[2]

Again, we find that " the divine Vishnu (the Sun-god) entered the body of that monarch, in consequence of his penances." And that, " for this reason, the entire universe offered divine worship to Prithu, numbered amongst the human gods " (demi-gods).[3]

It seems, therefore, that Prithu was worshipped during his lifetime as a personification of the Sun-god. It also seems that the title of Chakravarti raja must have been derived from the assumption of the chakra or discus, as a symbol, not only of universal dominion, but also of divine power as the Sun-god incarnate. Prithu is still worshipped as one of the Nāga demi-gods.

The great Daitya chief Hiranyakasipu, son of Kāsyapa, and raja of Pātala, also appears to have claimed divine powers; and Brāhmans, of the

[1] Muir, O.S.T., i. 302.

[2] Vishnu Purāna (Wilson), I. xiii. 101.

[3] Mahābhārata, Santi, Rajadharmānusasana, p. lix.

NĀGA RAJAS WITH CHAKRA AND SERPENT CANOPY,
AT RUINED TEMPLE NEAR BADARIWAR,

house of Bhrigu, seem to have ministered to him as a deity.[1]

We are told that Hiranyakasipu had brought the three worlds under his authority; had usurped the power of Indra, and exercised the functions of the Sun, of air, of the lord of the waters, of fire, and of the Moon.[2] In other words, the Daitya chief claimed power over the elements, as did other kings of Solar race.

Vāsuki is represented as holding in his hand, or sometimes in each hand, a discus or chakra. Other Nāga demi-gods are represented with a similar discus, so too is Sūrya the Sun-god, and so also is Vishnu.

The priests call the discus of Vāsuki, Nāga ka bhān. This, no doubt, represents the sun, as did the discus in the hand of Prithu, which has just been referred to.

In a very ancient Accadian poem, Merodach the Sun-god, says: "The sun of fifty faces (rays ?), the lofty weapon of my divinity, Ibear."

"The hero that striketh the mountains, the propitious sun of the morning, that is mine, Ibear."

"My mighty weapon, which, like an orb, smites in a circle the corpses of the fighters, Ibear."

And again: "That which makes the light come

[1] Vishnu Purāna, I. xvii. 129; I. xviii. 134.
[2] Ib. I. xvii. 126.

forth like day, god of the East, my burning power, I bear."[1]

Here the sun, or a representation of the sun, is evidently referred to. Moreover, in another ancient hymn or poem it is said : "The King, the shepherd of his people, may he hold the sun in his right hand; may he hold the moon in his left hand."[2]

From these passages it seems clear that Marduk or Merodach the Sun-god, and the early Babylonian kings, were shown as holding in their hands a representation of the sun. This was apparently in the form of an orb or a disk. It had, no doubt, the same signification as the discus or chakra, or Nāga ka bhān, of the Indian sun-god Sūrya, and of those Nāga rajas who claimed divine power as incarnations of the Sun-god. It was doubtless also the same as the disk beheld by Brahmā in the hand of Prithu, the Chakravarti raja, who, as we have just seen, was recognized by that deity as a personification of the Sun-god.

As in Babylonia, so too in India, the wheel or chakra represented the Sun. In the Rig Veda, Indra is said to have slain Bāla, by whirling round his vajra, or thunderbolt, as the sun turns round his wheel.[3]

[1] Chaldean Account of Genesis, 86.
Chaldean Magic, 162.
[2] Ib., 35. [3] Rig Veda, II. ii. 20.

VISHNU
WITH CHAKRA AND SEVEN-HEADED SERPENT.
From collection of the late Major E. Moor.

The idea of the Buddhist "wheel of the law" was doubtless derived from this wheel or chakra of the sun.

Krishna, who, as we shall see, claimed divine honours as an incarnation of the Sun-god, also carried a discus. This is represented sometimes as a mark of his divinity, and sometimes as a keen-edged weapon of destruction.

It seems probable that the disk of the Sun-god was sometimes confused with a sharp steel quoit, such as that carried by the Akālis or martial devotees of the Sikhs, which was an ancient weapon of war.

In the Mahābhārata, in one place, Pavaka or Agni is said to have given to Krishna a discus, which was a fiery weapon;[1] and in another place the discus is said to be made of iron.[2]

Again, we find: "The chief of the Yadus, that slayer of all foes, in anger instantly cut off the head of the ruler of Chedi by means of his discus."[3] Then, Krishna says that he launched the great powerful discus Sudarsana, "which reduceth to ashes in battle, Yakshas, Rakshasas, Dānavas and kings born in impure tribes."[4]

[1] Mahābhārata, Adi, Khāndavadaha, p. ccxxvii.
[2] Ib., Sauptika, p. xii.
[3] Ib., Sabha, Sisupālabadha, p. xlv.
[4] Mahābhārata, Arjunabigamana, p. xxii.

At the time of Krishna's death, his discus is said to have ascended to the sky.[1]

In the Purānas, the discus of Krishna is usually represented as a cutting weapon. By it the Asura Nāraka was cut in two,[2] and the king of Paundraka was cut in pieces.[3] The city of Kāsi, however, is said to have been burned by Sudarsana.[4]

Krishna, as already noted, claimed divine honours as the Sun-god personified, as did so many of the Solar rajas. Krishna, however, was not a king. He was the younger son of a chief of the Yādavas, and was a deified hero. He has now become one of the chief deities of the Hindu Pantheon, having in fact superseded Vishnu.

The Yādavas were of the Lunar line of Kshatriyas, yet Krishna claimed to be an incarnation of the Sun-god. It has been mentioned, however, that the Lunar line was separated from that of the Sun by religious differences only, and not by race.

We find that the Nāga chief Āryaka, of the race of Kauravya or Kuru, was great grandfather of Vasudeva, Krishna's father.[5]

Balarāma, elder brother of Krishna, is represented as having his head sheltered by the hoods

[1] Mahābhārata, Mausala, p. iv.
[2] Vishnu Purāna, V. xxix. 582.
[3] Ib. V. xxxiv. 599.
[4] Ib. V. xxxiv. 600.
[5] Mahābhārata, Adi, Sambhava, p. cxxviii.
Ib., Udyoga, Bhagavatyana, p. cii.

TEMPLE OF SESH NĀG,
DĀMAN, SĀRAJ

of many serpents.[1] This evidently refers to the serpent canopy, which distinguished the Nāga rajas. Moreover, Balarāma is said to have been an incarnation of Sesha Nāga,[2] and, at his death, his soul, in the form of a great serpent, escaped from his mouth.[3]

In the Bhagavadgita, Krishna describes himself as Vishnu, amongst the Adityas; and as the resplendent Sun amongst luminous bodies.[4] He is also said to be identical with the Sun,[5] and to be the genius (or deity) in the Solar disk.[6]

The title of Vāsudeva, which was claimed by Krishna, was assumed by other Solar chiefs—possibly by all who claimed paramount power. Thus Chakradhānu, "who took his birth from Sūrya," and who was also known as Kapila,[7] Kapila Vāsudeva,[8] and Kapila king of the Nāgas,[9] asserted his claim to universal dominion by seizing the sacrificial horse of Sagara. He also destroyed the sixty thousand sons of that monarch, who invaded Pātala in search of the horse.[10]

[1] Mahābhārata, Anusasana, Anusasanika, p. cxlvii.

[2] Ib.

[3] Vishnu Purāna, V. xxxvii. 611.

[4] Mahābhārata, Bhishma, Bhagavadgita, p. xxxv.

[5] Ib., Anusasana, Anusasanika, p. cxlix. [6] Ib.

[7] Ib., Udyoga, Bhagavatyana, p. cvii.

[8] Ib., Vana Tirthayatra, p. cvii.

[9] Ib., Vana, Titrhayatra, p. lxxxiv.

[10] Vishnu Purāna, IV. iv. 378.

The title of Vāsudeva was claimed, in Krishna's life-time, by a rival of his, "the heroic and mighty Vāsudeva, King of Pundra." This chief is said to have "represented himself as a divine personage and to have borne the signs of a Vāsudeva." He is also said to have fancied himself to be "the Vāsudeva," who had come down upon earth.[1] This king, who was defeated and killed by Krishna, evidently claimed divine honours, as the Sun-god personified.

Krishna appears to have more or less adopted Aryan customs. He was on very friendly terms with the Brahmans, and is represented as washing their feet.[2] He was, in fact, their champion. Krishna and his allies were engaged in frequent wars with other chiefs, many of whom are called Asuras. These were probably rulers of unregenerate tribes, who had not yet come under Brahmanical influence.

Amongst the kings despoiled by Krishna and his confederates, was the Nāga raja of Takshasilā, who lost Kurukshetra and the forest of Khāndava, or most of the country between the Sutlej and the Jumna rivers.[3]

In many of the conflicts referred to, Krishna was

[1] Mahābhārata, Sabha, Rajasuyarambha, p. xiv. Ib., Digvijaya, p. xxx.

[2] Ib., Sabha, Rajasuyaka, p. xxxv.

[3] Ib., Adi, Khāndavadaha, p. ccxxix.

assisted by Garuḍa, who is described as a supernatural being in the form of an eagle.

In front of the temples dedicated to Krishna, as Vishnu, is generally to be seen a pillar surmounted by the figure of an eagle with a human face, or of a man with the head of an eagle. This represents Garuḍa, the so-called vāhana, or carrier, of Krishna.

Who then was Garuḍa? We find, from the Mahābhārata, that the Garuḍas inhabited one of the provinces of Pātala. They are said to have been much favoured by Vishnu, or the Sun, whom they worshipped. A list of forty-eight Garuḍa chiefs is given, and it is said that only those are mentioned who have won distinction, by might, fame, and achievements.[1]

Garuḍa, or the eagle, therefore, was the totem of one of the Solar tribes of Pātala. These people were fierce and warlike, and they were engaged in frequent hostilities with their neighbours.

Garuḍa is described as tearing the bodies of the Yakshas, and devouring the Nishādas; also as destroying the elephant and the tortoise, which represent Solar tribes.[2]

Garuḍa is said to have attacked Indra, and to have carried off the Amrita.[3] Eventually he obtained

[1] Mahābhārata, Udyoga, Bhagavatyana, p. c.
[2] Ib., Adi, Astika, p. xxix.
[3] Ib., Adi, Astika, p. xxxiv.

a promise that the Nāgas should be his food, as he had complained that the Nishādas or aborigines, upon whom he had previously preyed, were not sufficient for him.

The story of the eagle devouring the serpents, therefore, is but a figurative description of inter-tribal warfare.

The Garuḍas are said to have been distinguished by the auspicious sign called "Srivatsa."[1] This was also an especial mark of Krishna. Moreover, the Garuḍas were under the leadership of that chief, and he adopted their totem as his ensign. In consequence of this, Krishna is poetically described as being carried, on his warlike expeditions, by the eagle.

This will serve to explain the various legends connecting the Nāgas with Garuḍa and with Krishna, and each of these with Vishnu or the Sun.

We have now seen, from abundant evidence, that originally the Nāgas were the Asuras or Serpas, and that these were of Solar race.

In later times, however, when Devas and Dānavas had all become Kshatriyas, and the events of former days had been to a great extent forgotten, Brāhmanical writers represented the Asuras as demons, who had assailed the Devas, as the Titans assailed the gods of Greece.

Still later the Asuras became the Nāgas of

[1] Mahābhārata, Udyoga, Bhagavatyana, p. c,

Pātala, which was described as a subterranean region, and which eventually became the Brāhmanical Hell.

The term Nāga was then applied to those descendants of the Solar tribes who had not become regenerate, but who retained the religion and customs of their forefathers. Now, these have all become more or less orthodox Hindus.

Indian folk-lore, however, is full of legends relating to the rajas and warriors of the serpent race. And the ancient festival of the Nāga-panchami is celebrated to this day, throughout India, in honour of the Nāga demi-gods.

CHAPTER III

WE have already seen that between the Vedic period and that described in the epic poems, great modifications occurred in the religion and social customs of the Indian people. Since the Epic period, further changes have taken place; so that the orthodox Hinduism of the present day differs much, not only from that described in the Veda, but also from that represented in the Mahābhārata. Religious vicissitudes have also occurred outside the Brahmanic pale. The Buddhist religion has become extinguished in India. Vast numbers of the people, too, have been converted—many of them forcibly—to the faith of Mohammed. Notwithstanding all this, however, many of the old deities still live. The Nāga rajas are worshipped as demigods; the sun, the cedar, and the serpent are held sacred; and Indra and his Devas have still their worshippers and their temples, as they had in the days described in the epic poems.

These old, and now unorthodox, divinities are the popular deities in most of the Himālayan valleys, and in many other parts of India.

In the mountainous country bordering upon Kashmir, and especially in the tract lying between the Chenab and Ravi rivers, a remnant of the Nāgas of the Mahābhārata still survives. These people have remained under more or less independent chiefs until comparatively recent times. They have escaped conversion to Islām, and they have saved their temples and their idols from the destructive zeal of Mohammedan iconoclasts, as well as from the almost equally destructive bigotry of the orthodox Brahman. Here the serpent-gods Sesha, Vāsuki, Bāsdeo, or Bāsak Nāg, Takshaka or Takht Nāg, and other Nāgas less known to fame, are still worshipped with their ancient rites. The forms of worship and the architecture of the temples have probably undergone little change since the days of the Mahābhārata. And the serpent-gods are worshipped now, as they were then, not as dangerous reptiles, nor as mere symbols, but as the deified rulers of an ancient people, whose tribal, or rather, perhaps, racial, emblem was the Nāga, or hooded serpent, and whose chief deity was the sun. These people do not call themselves Nāgas. That term was not a tribal name, but merely a distinctive term applied to those who reverenced the Nāga, or hooded serpent. The name by which they are now known is Takha. Taxiles, the ally of Alexander, was a Takha raja.

Amongst these people the Nāga—the cobra of the present day—was, and is, held sacred; and tradition says that the killing of one of these serpents, in olden times, involved the heaviest penalties. This, of course, is no longer the case, but I have heard men regret that the Nāg may now be killed in the country of Bāsdeo (Vāsuki). It is not that all serpents are regarded with veneration. Here, as elsewhere in India, the cobra alone is sacred. Other snakes may be killed without remorse. In one place only, so far as I am aware, is worship offered to any other serpent than the cobra. This is at the foot of the Rotang Pass, where, under an overhanging rock, offerings are made to some small harmless snakes, which are called "Nāg kiri." As this name shows, however, they are considered as representatives of the Nāga, which is rarely found at that altitude. Elsewhere, snakes of the same species are killed without scruple.

The Nāga temples are not, however, dedicated to the serpent, but to the Nāga rajas, the ancient rulers of the race, Sesh Nāg, Bāsak Nāg, Takht Nāg, Prithu Nāg, Karkota Nāg, Karsha Nāg, Sabīr Nāg, Sāntan Nāg, and many others, are all worshipped in human form. Each, however, has the hoods of three, five, seven, or more serpents, forming a canopy over his head, as shown by Fergusson in his plates of the Amarāwati sculptures.[1] In some places Nāgas of less note

[1] "Tree and Serpent Worship," plates xxiv., xliv., etc.

TEMPLE OF NĀGINI DEVI NEAR CHAMBA.

are represented as men, attended by snakes, but without the serpent-canopy. There are also temples dedicated to Nāgini Devis, who were the wives of Nāga chiefs.

In some temples, the images of the Nāga demigods are draped in white calico, so that only the heads are visible.

As elsewhere explained, since the Asuras became Kshatriyas their souls have become Devas, and those of their wives have become Devis. Hence, there have been no Nāgas or Nāginis in recent times. Those, whose shrines remain, belong to the distant past.

Within each temple is the image of the Nāga raja, with the serpent-canopy over his head. There are also many iron trisulas, or tridents, and representations of snakes in iron and stone, which have been placed there by worshippers as votive offerings. Besides these, are a lamp, a dish for burning incense, and the sacred sūngal, gājā, or iron scourge, This is the exact counterpart of that represented in the hand of the Egyptian Osiris.

Besides the temples already mentioned, small shrines containing rudely sculptured representations of serpents are numerous ; as also are similar representations of the Nāga, placed under trees. To all these offerings are made.

At the Nāga temples the representation of the

sun occupies a prominent position, being carved upon the roof and other parts of the building. In these primitive shrines I could discover no trace of any connection between the Nāga and the Phallus. The worship is simply that of the Nāga demigods, as descendants of the Sun, and ancestors of the Solar race. The Devas, too, whose temples are found throughout the Himālaya, are deified Kshatriyas, and ancestors of the people. The rites and ceremonial at the Nāga temples are essentially the same as those at the temples of the Devas. And it is very unlikely that any important change has occurred, in this respect, since the ancient times when Swārga was occupied by the Nāgas and the Devas. In each case, goats and sheep are sacrificed, votive offerings are made, lights and incense are burned, the smoke of cedar is used for purification and protection against evil spirits, circumambulation of the temple takes place, and the deity is consulted through his inspired prophet. This representative of the deity sometimes passes through the fire, or inhales the smoke of burning cedar, and almost always does penance with the sūngal or iron scourge. Music and dancing form an important part of the ceremonial. The musicians are often of aboriginal race, and being therefore considered as of lower caste, are not allowed to approach within a

INTERIOR OF TEMPLE OF BĀSDEO,
GHĀTI, BADARIWAR.

certain distance of the shrine. The dancing at the temples and in ceremonial processions is confined to men. I have seen worshippers dancing before the litter, in which the representation of the deity was travelling, as David danced before the Ark.

In most of the temples to Vāsuki or Bāsdeo in the Chenab̠ valley there is, besides the figure of the Nāga raja, a representation of his Wuzir, who is called Jimuta-vāhana. Legend says that Bāsdeo was engaged in war with Garuḍa, and that, on one occasion, the Nāga chief was surprised by the enemy and had a narrow escape. In fact, he was saved only by the devotion of his minister, who gave his own life to save that of his master. This probably means that Jimuta-vāhana was killed in covering the retreat of the raja. Bāsdeo escaped to the Kailās Kūnd, a mountain lake some 13,000 feet above the sea, between the Chenab and Rāvi valleys. Meantime an army was raised, by which Garuḍa was defeated. The Nāga raja, in his gratitude, ordered that in future Jimuta-vāhana should be worshipped in the same temple with himself. It would seem from this that Vāsuki, like other Solar kings, received divine honours during his lifetime.

The legend, just referred to, seems to relate to some of the struggles between the unregenerate and the Aryanized tribes. It is probably founded on fact. At all events, a great festival is held annually at the Kailās Kūnd, which is attended by all the population of the surrounding country. It seems probable that this legend suggested the story of Jimuta-vāhana in the Kathā Sarit Sagara;[1] and also the plot of the Nāga Nanda, which is in fact the same story dramatized. In each case the events occur in the reign of Vāsuki; in each case the name of the hero is Jimuta-vāhana; in each case his home is in the Himālaya; and in each case he gives himself up to Garuḍa, to save the life of another. Here, however, the resemblance ceases. The drama has a Buddhist complexion. Vāsuki is represented as being obliged to provide one of his subjects, daily, to be eaten by Garuda. The place of one of the victims is taken by Jimuta-vāhana, who is partially devoured. Garuḍa then finds out his mistake, releases him, promises to eat no more human beings, and restores to life the Nāgas he had previously consumed.

In connection with this subject it is interesting to note that, according to the Chinese Buddhist pilgrim I-tsing, the great raja Silāditya kept all the best writers, especially poets, at his court, and even joined in their recitals. The king would take the part of Jimuta-vāhana, and

[1] Kathā Sarit Sagara (Tawney), i. 186.

DISTANT VIEW OF KAILAS KUND.

transform himself into a Nāga, amid songs and instrumental music.[1]

In Gurhwal and Kemāon I have not met with any representation of Jimuta-vāhana in the Nāga temples, which are numerous. The legend, therefore, is probably local.

It has already been mentioned that in some of his temples Bāsdeo or Vāsuki is represented as holding in his hand, or sometimes in each hand, a disc or chakra, which the priests call "Nāga ka bhān." Sūrya the Sun-god is represented as holding a similar object. So also are Indru Nāga (Nahush) and other Nāga rajas. This disc evidently represents the Sun.

Most of the temples of the Nāga rajas are built of massive logs of cedar, and are sheltered in fine old cedar groves. In the Chenab valley many of the grandest trees were, sad to say, cut up into railway sleepers not long ago. The cedar, kelu, or deodāra (tree of the gods) is sacred throughout the Hindu Kush and the Himālaya, as it was in ancient Babylonia, and the neighbouring countries.

Branches of this tree are burned at sacrifices to keep off evil spirits, and the smoke is inhaled by the inspired prophets with the same object. It was not only amongst the people of the hills

[1] "Buddhist Annals of Western World" (Beal), i. 210 (note).

that the cedar was sacred, for at the great horse sacrifice of Yudishthira two of the sacrificial posts were of deodāra.[1] At the Aswamedha of Dasaratha also, two of the posts were of this sacred tree.[2] The wood in both cases must have been brought from the Himālaya, as the cedar does not grow in the plains of India. So highly venerated is this tree, that some years ago, when the raja of Mandi, in the Beas valley, leased the right to cut deodar timber in his dominions to a firm of contractors, his people rose in rebellion. They said the land no doubt was the raja's, but the trees belonged to the gods. The raja had to apply to the British Government for protection against his angry subjects.

It may be observed that the Kashmir shawl-pattern is a conventional representation of the *Cedrus deodara*.

Several other trees are sacred in the Himālaya, notably the juniper and the ash, but none is held in the same degree of reverence as the cedar.

The different serpent-gods, with their insignia, and attended by their priests and office-bearers, visit each other's festivals. The Devas, also, visit each other in the same way. These festivals are held at all the principal temples. In front of these, there is usually an open grassy space, surrounded

[1] Mahābhārata, Aswamedha, Anugita, p. lxxxviii. 222.

[2] Ramāyana, I. xxxii.

TEMPLE OF KARĀUN NĀG,
KŪLŪ.

by seats arranged somewhat in the form of an amphitheatre. Here each caste and family has its allotted position, according to ancient custom.

Besides the regular festivals, gatherings occur at the temples on other important occasions, as when the people meet to consult their gods through the medium of the inspired prophets. Such assemblages usually occur in case of war, famine, or pestilence. Sometimes several deities meet in conclave, each being represented by his temple officials. Such a convocation is probably referred to in the passage in the Mahābhārata, which tells us that the gods (Devas), having assembled on the banks of the Sāraswati, there installed the excellent Nāga Vāsuki as king of all the serpents.[1]

The priests of most of these temples, whether of the Nāgas or of the Devas, are Kshatriyas, or Khuttris as they are called in the vernacular. In this, we have a survival of ancient customs existing in the far-off days when the Kshatriya chief offered his own sacrifices.

At some of the temples, however, the priests are so-called "desi," or local, Brahmans. These belong to none of the known Brahmanical clans, and are not recognized by them. They probably are members of families who, from long connection

[1] Mahābhārata, Salya, Gudāyudhya, p. xxvii. 149.

with the temples, have acquired priestly dignity. In many places they intermarry with the Khuttris. In this, however, they only follow the example of ancient rishis, such as Sakra and Chyavana.

Orthodox Brahmans may sometimes be found officiating at these unorthodox temples, but this is very rarely the case. When it does occur, the position of the Brahman is but a subordinate one.

Whether, however, there be a Brahman priest or not, there is always an inspired prophet, who is the medium of communication between the deity and the people. In some cases, when many of the worshippers are of lower caste, or of aboriginal descent, there is also a prophet of lower grade, called " lamahāta," who passes on to them the communications received through the inspired representative of the deity.

The inspired prophet is known by several titles, as chela, gūr-chela, banahāta, dharmi, dangarīah, or, in some instances, as Rā. He is generally a Kshatriya. but sometimes, though rarely, he is a desi-Brahman. I have never known an orthodox Brahman act in this capacity, but I have seen one of them, as priest, incensing the chela while in the condition of inspired frenzy.

The chela or banahāta is not elected, but is supposed to become possessed, or " seized," as the expression is, by the deity. Should he, how-

CHELA OF KATYŪR DEO, KAMAON.

ever, be considered an improper person, he is called before the village elders, who, in solemn conclave, decide upon his claims. The office is not hereditary. The chela, when he receives his call, must separate from his family; must lead a celibate life; must eat no food which has not been prepared with his own hands; must sleep on the ground; and must not wear shoes. In some cases the chela is allowed to live in his own house, but the other rules appear to be always enforced. In most places the chela, when under the divine influence, must not be touched by any other person.

When, as is rarely the case, the worship at a Nāga, or Deva, temple is conducted by a Brahman priest, he has no authority over the chela or over the temple property, nor has he any power to regulate the festivals, or to make any demands from the worshippers. The temple management is in the hands of the council of elders, guided by the will of the deity, as announced by the prophet when under the influence of the divine afflatus. The chela then represents the deity, and is spoken of as the deity. It is probable that when in the epic poems we read of the commands of Indra, or other divinities, the utterances of the inspired prophet are referred to. As may well be imagined, the influence of these men, for good or for evil, is very great. There can, I think, be little doubt that many an apparently inexplicable outburst of fanaticism has been caused by the raving of these prophets. Sir G. Robertson mentions that a bloody war between two Kāfir clans was caused by the utterances of a "pshur,"[1] which is the title given to the inspired prophets in the valleys of the Hindu Kush. It seems to me at least probable that the mad attack upon a British force at Manipur a few years ago, followed by the murder of several officers, had a similar origin. I was assured, by a very intelligent chief, that no one dared to disobey the orders of the deity received through the inspired chela. He added that should any one do so, some dreadful calamity would certainly happen.

In the Himālaya, the inspired prophet at the temples of Devas or Nāgas, whatever may be his local title, is not a sorcerer or magician. Unlike the orthodox Brahman, he does not pretend to any power over the divinity he represents, or any other, either in consequence of his austerities, or by means of mantras, or through any rites or ceremonial. He is merely the mouthpiece of the deity. So far as I have seen, too, the chela does not wear any fantastic costume or grotesque ornaments. He wears the same dress as the other villagers, except that he must never wear shoes. The chelas, however, of some of the Devis, and of

[1] "Kāfirs of the Hindu Kush," p. 418.

CHELA OF SHAMŪ DEO, THĀT, KAMAON.

a few of the Nāgas, wear a red cap. This is of the same shape as those of the other villagers. The only difference is in colour. The prophet is of course treated with great respect, but his emoluments are very small. He has a right to the head of every victim sacrificed, and sometimes he receives an extra portion. He often, too, receives small contributions of grain at harvest time; and, if the temple has an endowment, he has a small sum from that source. In most cases, however, he derives his subsistence, mainly, from his own land.

The foregoing does not in all particulars agree with descriptions, which have been given, of the unorthodox rites practised in the south of India. Of these latter I have no personal knowledge. What I have just said must be considered as relating to Northern India only.

That all these men believe in their own inspiration it would probably be too much to say, but some of them certainly seem to do so. I have known several of them. I once asked a man, whose father had been a chela, why he had not been inspired. He said, simply, that the Deo had never come to him. He seemed to have no doubt as to the reality of his father's inspiration, or the possibility of his own.

As to the worshippers, the sincerity of their faith is often shown by the severity of their penances. I have seen a man apply the sũngal, or iron scourge, to his own bare back and shoulders, till the blood ran down in streams, and formed a pool upon the ground. The punishment was most severe.

At sacrifices the chela, as already mentioned, inhales the smoke of burning cedar, and in some cases he drinks the warm blood from the neck of the decapitated victim. Sometimes, too, he jumps into or over the sacrificial fire. He always applies to his own back, and sometimes to those of the worshippers, the iron scourge which has just been referred to.

This application of the sũngal, to the backs of the worshippers, is sometimes merely a ceremonial one, no blood being drawn. But when the scourge is used by the penitents themselves the punishment is very real.

This scourge, as already mentioned, appears to be the exact counterpart of that represented in the hands of Osiris and of several of the Egyptian deities. It is made entirely of iron, and varies in weight from about three to five pounds. It has usually three, but sometimes five, lashes. Each of these is made up of two or three long links and a broad lancet-shaped blade at the extremity. This somewhat resembles in shape the broad piece of leather at the end of the thong of a Tartar whip. It occurred to me

EGYPTIAN GOD KHONSU
With Scourge similar to Sūngal.

SUNGAL OR GĀJĀ.

that this scourge might be the same as the "aspaheastra," or "sraoshôcharana," of the Zoroastrains.[1] But the late esteemed Professor Darmesteter, to whom I mentioned this, considered that the Zoroastrian scourge had thongs of leather. Be this as it may, it seems probable that they were but different forms of the same instrument. The mode of use, and the expiatory effect, were the same in each case.

Some years ago I was invited by the Chāk, or local chief, of Barmāor, in the valley of the Rāvi, to attend a great sacrifice to Kailang Nāg. The object of the sacrifice was to obtain fine weather for the sowing, which had been delayed by storms. Kailang, like other Nāga demigods, is supposed to control the weather.

On my arrival, I found the people assembled on the open grassy space in front of the temple. The men and boys sat together, the women and girls being at a little distance. Soon the music struck up, and some of the men and boys began to dance in a circle, the chela dancing in the centre. After a time the music became wilder and the dance more energetic. Some of the men when tired sat down, and others took their places. The chela continued dancing, and he applied the sūngal to his own back and shoulders and to those of some of the other dancers. Some of

[1] Vendidad (S.B.E.), Far. xiv. 8.

the men then applied another similar scourge to their own backs, with great effect, amid shouts of "Kailang Mahārāj kī jāi!" (Victory to the great King Kailang). Then, all being ready, the victim (a ram) was led out, and having shown, by shivering, that it was acceptable to the deity, its head was struck off. The body was immediately lifted up by several men, and the chela, seizing upon it, drank the blood as it spouted from the neck, amid renewed shouts of "Kailang Mahārāj kī jāi!" The carcase was thrown down upon the ground, and the head, with a burning coal upon it, placed before the threshold of the temple. The dancing was then renewed, and became more violent, until the chela gasped out "Kailang āya" (Kailang has come). All then became silent, and the prophet announced that the sacrifice was accepted, and that the season would be favourable. This was received with a storm of shouts of "Kailang Mahārāj kī jāi!" and the chela sank down upon the ground exhausted. Water was poured over him, and he was vigorously fanned till he showed signs of revival. The assembly then began to disperse.

Kailang Nāg is one of the deities, to whom human sacrifices are said to have been offered in former days. There are many temples, in the Himālaya, at which human beings are said to have been offered, in times of drought and

BRIHĀRŪ NĀG,
SĀRAJ
(Chela in foreground)

threatened famine. One of these, near the Sāch Pass, is dedicated to a Nāgini known as "Amā Nāga," who has the reputation of having often refused to give rain " until she had eaten men." Certain villages, in turn, supplied the victims.

Kailang Nāg had a shrine in the valley of the Chandra-Bhāga river. Tradition says that there human sacrifices were frequent. At last it came to the turn, to provide the victim, of a widow, who had an only child—a son. The boy was accordingly devoted.

The mother, in great distress, was sitting near the temple, when a Buddhist monk came by, and, on hearing the woman's story, offered to take the place of the victim.

Next day was fixed for the sacrifice. There was a great gathering, and the monk was present. He said, however, that he did not wish to be killed by any one but the Nāga; and that he would sit at the temple, until the deity came to devour him. This was agreed to. After sitting there for some days, without anything happening to him, the monk persuaded the people that the Nāga did not wish men to be sacrificed. From that time, no more human victims were offered to Kailang.

At these temples, either of Nāgas or Devas, votive offerings are made, as in the Catholic Church. These are in fulfilment of vows made during sickness, danger, or misfortune. Thus, a man may promise a trident to Vāsuki or Takshaka; or a plough, a sword, or a bullock-yoke to the tutelary Deva of the village. These are generally represented by small models, which are placed in the temple. Sometimes, however, the object actually devoted is given up to the deity. I have seen a spinning-wheel placed in a small shrine, which was scarcely large enough to hold it. In this old form of Hinduism the offerings are made to the gods, not to the Brahmans.

Around most of the old temples, either of Devas or of Nāgas, are arranged a number of stone tablets, like small tombstones, on each of which is rudely carved the figure of a man, or those of a man and woman. These are the monuments of deceased villagers, and correspond to the gravestones in our churchyards. As the dead are burned, there are no graves.

Similar memorials are sometimes placed at the village spring, at the crossing of a stream, or in some other frequented place; and sometimes, in addition to the tablet, some work of public utility, as a resting-place for travellers, a fountain, or a bridge over a stream, is erected in memory of the wealthier villagers.

The monuments to the rajas are on a larger scale, and upon them were, formerly, sculptured

MONUMENTS TO RAJAS OF MANDI, BEAS VALLEY.

the representations of the wives and dependants who accompanied the chief to the other world.

At some of the temples of the Devas a pole or mast, called dhuj (dhwaja), is erected. This is a pine-tree stripped of its branches, and it is renewed yearly, the old one being burned. As its name denotes, this is the standard of the deity. It is referred to in the Mahābhārata, where Indra directs the King of Chedi to set up an Indra-dhwaja.[1] In processions a smaller dhuj is often carried by the chela. On the Indus, and other Panjāb rivers, the boatmen place a pole surmounted by a tuft of hair at the bows or at the masthead of their boats, as the dhuj of Khwaja Khizr, which is the Mussulman name for Varuna, the ancient sea-god.

Pilgrimages are made to the temples of Devas and Nāgas as well as to those of the Devis and Nāginis. These are usually in fulfilment of vows, or to ask some favour of the deity, and are often undertaken by married women without children. These pilgrimages are frequently made by night, and in some localities it is customary to make a mark, at every few yards, upon a stone or other object by the roadside. These marks are called "likhnū," and are made with a mixture of rice-flour and water. They are a sort of record that the pilgrimage has been duly performed.

[1] Mahābhārata, Adi, Adivansāvatārana, p. lxii. 173.

The Devis were in most cases the wives of Kshatriya chiefs, who became "sati," or were burned with the bodies of their husbands; but the term is now applied to almost all female divinities. The Nāginis, as already mentioned, were the wives of the Nāga rajas.

These Devas and Nāgas were the ancestors of the present Hindu people, and they were the popular deities of the epic poems, and of the early Buddhist legends. It was over them that Indra reigned, and over them, in the Himālaya, he reigns still. Yet, by the orthodox Brahman, these divinities are now considered as demons; and they have been so described by European writers, who derived their information from Brahmanical sources. The worship of ancestors, or of deified human beings, has prevailed throughout the world, and even now it is far from being extinct. Arhats and rishis, saints and angels are still reverenced, and even Mohammedanism has its Pirs.

TEMPLE OF SAVIR NĀG,
SŪILL VALLEY.

CHAPTER IV

THE worshippers of the sun and the serpent, whose religious rites and ceremonial have just been described, are a remnant of a tribe, or group of tribes, once very powerful but now broken and scattered. They are known, in different localities, as Takha, Katha, Kathak, Kāthia, Kathūria, and Kator, with other variants. Some of these mutations of name seem to be due to the practice of inversion, so common in the dialects of northern India, by which, for instance, the name of the city of Luknow becomes Nuklow in the vulgar tongue. Most of the Takhas, who still retain that name, and still worship the Nāga demi-gods their ancestors, are to be found, in the Panjāb, in the valleys of the Chināb, Ravi and Beas rivers. These are fine-looking men, many of whom serve in our Indian regiments. The Kashmir armies have always been largely recruited from them. In speech and in physiognomy there is nothing to distinguish the Takhas from other Rajput tribes in the Panjāb. They are included, by the bard Chand, amongst the thirty-six royal races of India.[1]

The worship of the Nāga was not confined to the Takhas. As already noted, the hooded serpent was held sacred by all who claimed Solar descent. The Takhas, however, were amongst the most powerful, and most widely spread, of those Indian peoples who clung to the religion and customs of their forefathers.

From the Mahābhārata we learn that Takshaka, the great Nāga chief, and his son the mighty Aswasena, lived in Kurukshetra and Khāndhava;[2] and that Takshasilā was their northern capital. Takshaka, however, is also called Takshaka Vaisāliya,[3] from Visālā or Ujaini, which city must, therefore, have been included in his dominions. In fact, the rule of the Takha chiefs seems to have extended from the Hindu Kush and Himālaya southwards, over Sind, the Panjāb and a great part of what is now called Rajputana. Most of these possessions were lost long ago. The last Takha chiefs, to whom a shadow of independence remained, held out in the Chināb valley until they were dispossessed by Golab Sing of Kashmir.

According to local tradition, the Takhas of the Panjāb held the Himālaya from the Indus to the

[1] "Annals of Rajasthan," i. 75.

[2] Mahābhārata, Adi, Paushya, p. iii.

[3] Atharva Veda, viii. ix. 2.

SHIB CHARRAN, TAKHA CHIEF OF KALENI, AND HIS SON.

Sutlej. This appears to be confirmed by the great number of shrines, sacred to the Nāga demi-gods, which exist there; and by the many remains of ancient fortifications, ascribed by the people to Takha chiefs, who are said to have held the country before the rajas. By this is meant, before the present ruling Rajput families. Much of the land in this tract is still held by Takhas; and the ancient Takari alphabet, which takes its name from this people, is still in use from Bamian and the Kābul valley to Nepāl.[1]

In the seventh century the Chinese pilgrim Hiouen Tsiang found the kingdom of Takha extending from the Indus to the Beas; the cities of Sakala and Multān being included within its boundaries.[2] We learn, too, from the Chuchnama, that Jaisya, son of Dahir, king of Sind, flying from the victorious Arab invaders, in the eighth century, took refuge in the country of Takhia.[3]

Early in the tenth century we find that Shankara Varma, king of Kashmir, defeated Alakhana, king of Gurjara or Guzrat, and took from him Takha, which was then a part of his dominions. The country was restored to the Takha chief, who became a dependant of Kashmir.[4]

[1] Cunningham, Arch. Reports, ii. 9.
[2] Hiouen Tsaing, Beal, i. 165. [3] Elliot, i. 178.
[4] Rajataraṇgini, Stein, v. 150, 151.

Besides the Takha kingdom in the Himālaya, which, as already noted, extended from Kashmir to the Sutlej, the country west of the Indus, as far as Kābul, was ruled by a branch of the same people, generally known as Kator, who will be referred to later. Again, the tract extending from the Sutlej to Nepāl was occupied by another offshoot of the same race, who were called Katūr, Kathūria, or Kathiūr.

The dominions of the Kathūria rajas, like those of the Takhas, extended far into the plains, and included the district now known as Rohilkand, but then called Kathēr.

The Kathūrias, like the Takhas or Kathas, claimed descent from the Sun, through the Nāga demi-gods.

At Badariwar, in the valley of the Chināb, the principal temples are sacred to Bāsdeo or Vāsuki, as ancestor of the Takhas; and at Josimath, in the Alaknanda valley, which was the residence of the early Kathūria rajas, the most ancient temple is dedicated to Bāsdeo, as ancestor of the Kathūrias.[1]

The Takari alphabet was, and still is, in use in Gurhwāl and Kamāon; and the temples to the Nāga demi-gods, which are very numerous, are sacred to the same deities as are those in the Panjāb. Airi or Airāvata, however, seems to take

[1] Gazetteer N.W.P. (Kamāon), i. 467.

INTERIOR OF TEMPLE OF AIRI DEO,
DŌL, KAMAON.

the place of Takshaka. This may be owing to Takshaka having been a Panjāb chief; while "the serpents, subjects of King Airāvata, splendid in battle," seem to have lived on the northern bank of the Ganges, where there are said to be many dwelling-places of Nāgas.[1] Airi, like other Nāga demi-gods, is represented by the trisul or trident, and his shrines are sheltered in groves of cedar.

Temples to Devas are also numerous in Gurhwāl and Kamāon; and the rites and ceremonial practised at the shrines, both of Devas and Nāgas, are similar to those in use in the worship of these deities in the Panjāb, which have already been described.

According to local tradition, Sankara Acharya, who came from the Dekhan with a large following, was favourably received by one of the Kāthuria rajas; and, with his aid, drove the Buddhists out of Gurhwāl, Kamāon and Nepāl.

The most important religious establishments were then made over to Sankara's followers, whose descendants still enjoy them.

The annals of Nepāl fully confirm the Kamāon legends as to Sankara's persecution of the Buddhists, and relate how he made the Bikshus offer bloody sacrifices, and married the monks to the nuns.[2] Tradition also says that the great temple

[1] Mahābhārata, Adi, Pausya, p. iii.

[2] Nepāl, Wright, 119, 120.

of Vishnu at Badarinath was built by the raja for the Brahmanical reformer. To this day the Rāwal, and other principal priests of this temple, are Namburi Brāhmans from southern India.[1]

Legend says that Sankara told the raja that he would neither eat nor drink until one hundred temples had been built to Vishnu. The raja gave the necessary orders, and the temples were built in groups. They are still standing, but it is said that most of them were never used for worship.

Some of the Kathūria rajas, like other Solar chiefs who have been referred to, appear to have assumed the title of Vāsudeva or Bāsdeo; and they probably also claimed the divine honours which belonged to it. In an inscription in the old temple to Bāsdeo at Josimath, one of the Kathūria rajas is called "Sri Bāsdeo Girirāj Chakra Churamani."[2]

Several authorities mention that Rajpāl, raja of Indraprastha or Delhi, invaded Kamāon, where he was defeated and killed by a chief called Sakwanta or Shakaditya. The conqueror seized upon Indraprastha, and reigned there for fourteen years. He was then overthrown and killed by Vikramaditya, whose capital was Ujāini.[3]

[1] Report on Source of the Ganges, As. Res. viii.

[2] Gaz. N.W.P. (Kamāon), 467.

[3] "Annals of Rajasthan," i. 51; Ward, Hist. Hindus, i. 21. Ind. Arch. Reports, i. 137, 138; Gaz. N.W.P. (Kamāon), i. 411.

TEMPLE OF THE SUN AT KATARMAL, KAMAON.

Sakwanta was apparently one of the Kathūrias, who had then been rulers of Kamāon for a very long period, as we shall presently see.

It is recorded by Ferishta that during the time of anarchy which followed upon the death of raja Bhōj Puār, the throne of Kanōj was seized by Bāsdeo,[1] who is described as a conqueror from the country of Kuttair, that is Kamāon.[2] Who this Bāsdeo was is uncertain. As, however, he came from Kamāon, it is probable that he was one of the Kathūrias. Bāsdeo is said to have reigned at Kanōj for seventy years. At his death, his sons quarrelled over the succession; and Rāmdeo Rhātor, who had been commander of the army of Bāsdeo, seized the throne.[3]

After some time, Rāmdeo attacked the Sawalik chiefs. He was opposed by the raja of Kamāon, who "had inherited his country and his throne from a long line of ancestors, who had reigned upwards of two thousand years."[4] In a great battle, which lasted from sunrise to sunset, the Kamāon raja was defeated, and fled to the hills. Rāmdeo, having compelled him to give his daughter in marriage, left the raja in possession of his country.[5]

[1] Ferishta, Briggs, I. lxxviii.
[2] "Annals of Rajasthan," i. 54.
[3] Ferishta, Briggs, I. lxxviii.
[4] Ib. I. lxxviii. [5] Ib. I. lxxviii.

The Kathūria dynasty continued to rule in Kamāon for many generations after this, for an inscription was found, at Dwāra, of Ananta Pāla Deva Katiūr, the date of which corresponded to A.D. 1122.[1]

Some minor chiefs still remain, who claim descent from the Kathūrias. All ancient remains, in Gurhwāl and Kamāon, are ascribed by the people to this dynasty; and several of the former chiefs of this line are still worshipped as Devas.

[1] Gazetteer N.W.P. (Kamāon), 520.

CHAPTER V

THE people with whom Alexander first came into contact, after crossing the Indus, were the serpent-worshipping Takhas or Kathas. The Taxila of the Greeks was the ancient Nāga capital Takshasilā ; and, as already mentioned, Taxiles or Omphis was a Takha chief.

Takhas or Kathas are still the principal land-holders in the country round the ruins of the great Nāga city, which is locally known as Katha-des. These people, who are now Mohammedans, maintained a state of semi-independence until comparatively recent times.

Adjoining the territory of Takshasilā, to the north and east, were the serpent-worshipping countries of Uraga, or Urasa, and Abissara. Beyond these was Kashmir. This country was, according to its own historians,[1] under the protection of Nila Nāga and other serpent deities from the earliest times. One of the principal dynasties, too, which afterwards ruled Kashmir was descended from the Nāga demi-god Karkotaka.[2]

[1] Rajatarangini, Stein, i. 26, 27, 28. [2] Ib. iii. 529, 530.

Every spring, stream and lake, in this country, was sacred to one or other of the Nāga deities. And Abul Fuzl tells us that in seven hundred places representations of the serpent-gods, carved in stone, were set up and worshipped.

At the same time, according to the same authority, there were only forty-five shrines sacred to Siva, sixty-four to Vishnú, three to Brahmā, and twenty-two to Durgah.[1] The Nāga demi-gods, therefore, were by far the most popular deities.

The sculptures referred to have been destroyed by Mohammedan iconoclasts, but the sites still retain the names of the serpent deities to whom they were sacred.

In almost all of the neighbouring Hindu states the people are of Solar race, and the Nāga demi-gods are worshipped as ancestral deities.

We have already seen that, in Vedic times, the Āryas or Devas were opposed, on the borders of India, by tribes to whom the term Ahi or serpent was applied. We have seen, too, that these were apparently of the race represented by the Azi-dahāka of the Zend Avesta. At a later period we find descendants of this serpent race still ruling in Kābul and in the neighbouring country, as tributaries of the Persian empire.

We learn from Firdūsi, who is confirmed by Mirkhond and other Persian authorities, that Zāl

[1] Ayeen Akbary, Gladwin, ii. 137.

TEMPLE OF SANTAN NĀG.
CHINĀB VALLEY.

son of Sām, who was ruler of Zābulistan under the king of Persia, paid a visit to Mihrāb, chief of Kābulistan, who was descended from the family of Zahāk. Zāl fell in love with Rudābeh, the daughter of Mihrāb, but the Mobeds, or Zoroastrian priests, who were consulted, knowing that Mihrāb was of serpent race, would not sanction the marriage. The matter was referred to Sām. This chief does not seem to have made any objection, and his influence was sufficient to obtain the consent of the Persian king, although that ruler had previously ordered the destruction of Kābul by fire and sword, and the slaughter of the descendants of Zahāk.[1]

The great Persian hero Rūstam was the son of Zāl, and his mother was Rudābeh, the daughter of the serpent chief.[2] Mirkhond, in describing this relationship of Rūstam to the chief of Kābulistan, says that, in consequence of it, Rūstam was called "Kābuli" by the nobles at the Persian court.[3] Rūstam, who was killed at Kābul, was succeeded as ruler of Kābul and Zābul by his son Ferimarz, who held the country until he was killed by the Persian king.[4]

Other parts of the mountainous country, now known as Afghānistan, were occupied by descend-

[1] Shahnama, Atkinson, 77. Rauzat-us-Safā, Shea, 171.

[2] Shahnama, Atkinson, 77.

[3] Rauzat-us-safā, Shea, 171, 195.

[4] Ib. 349, 353.

ants of Azi or Zahāk down to comparatively recent times.

Malcolm, in his history of Persia, says that the princes of Ghor derived their proud descent from Zahāk, and boasted that their ancestors had successfully opposed Feridūn.[1]

Ferishta tells us that "the race of Zahāk, one after another, succeeded to the chieftainship of Ghor until the time of the Prophet." [2] We learn also, from the same authority, that the genealogy of the kings of Ghor, according to the most authentic historians, could be traced upwards by the names for three and twenty generations.[3]

Minhāju-s Sirāj, who came from Ghor to India in A.H. 624 (A.D. 1227), and whose father was Kazi to the army of the great Mahomed Ghori, commences his history of the Ghorian kings with a genealogical list, which traces their descent back through Zahāk to Noah.[4] Whatever may be thought of this long pedigree, there was evidently a general agreement among historians that the kings of Ghor, in the mountains of Afghānistan, were descended from Zahāk.

It seems, therefore, that the ruling family of Kābul, in the time of Rūstam, and the chiefs of

[1] Malcolm, Hist. Pers., I. 347.
[2] Ferishta, Dow, I. 124; Ib. Briggs, i. 162.
[3] Ib. i. 124; Ib. i. 163.
[4] Tabakat-i Nasiri (Elliot, ii. 282, note).

Ghor, as late as the thirteenth century, claimed to be of serpent race. So that in the principal states of Afghānistan, that is in the very country in which the Āryas encountered Ahi, the serpent chief of the Rig Veda, the ruling families claimed to be descended from Azi, the serpent chief of the Zend Avesta.

We shall see later that the people of the country between Kābul and Kashmir, down to the time of the Mohammedan invasion, still worshipped the Nāga demi-gods.

In the Pahlavi Kārnām-i Artakshir-i Pāpakān it is mentioned that the Persian King Artakshir in the first half of the third century was defeated more than once, and his camp taken, by Haftan Bokht. This chief, who was ruler of Kirmān and lord of the dragon, worm, or serpent,[1] was eventually defeated and killed. The ruins of his fortress of Guzārān are near the town of Bam, not far from the frontier of Baluchistan. The Bam fort is still known as Kut-i-Kirm, or fort of the worm or serpent.[2]

Other traces of the serpent race remain in the neighbouring country. In Baluchistan is the Koh-i-Mārān, or the mountain of serpents,[3] which doubtless took its name from the race of Zahāk.

And one of the legends, relating to the building

[1] J.R.A.S. January, 1898, 178.

[2] Ib. October, 1902, 944-5.

[3] Baluchistan, Hughes, 5.

of Herāt, says that this fortress was founded by a daughter of Zahāk.[1]

Notwithstanding the conversion of the people to the Mohammedan faith, traditions connected with the serpent race still remain in the wild country between Persia and the Indian border. Near Mazar, in northern Afghānistan, is the village of Gor-i-Mār, or grave of the serpent, where a great serpent is said to have been killed by Ali.[2] Amongst the Kafirs of the Hindu Kush, also, there is a tradition that the Bashgul valley was once held by a great serpent, who devoured travellers passing that way, and who was killed by Imra or Indra.[3]

The first clear descriptions we have, of the country between Kābul and the Indus, are those of the Chinese pilgrims who visited India as the holy land of Buddhism. Of these, Fah Hian arrived in India about A.D. 400, and seems to have travelled by way of Bālti and the upper Indus valley.

This pilgrim says: "Crossing the river Sinto (Indus), we come to Wuchang, where commences Northern India."

Wuchang, or Udyāna, included the valley of the Swat river and much of the neighbouring country.

Fah Hian goes on to say that the language and dress of the people, and their food and drink, are

[1] Rehatsek, Ind. Ant. April, 1874.

[2] Yate, N. Afghānistan, 315.

[3] "Kafirs of the Hindu Kush," 388.

the same as in mid-India.[1] They were, therefore, an Indian race. He further describes the religion of Buddha as very flourishing,[2] and mentions that Sakya visited this country, to convert a wicked Nāga.[3]

The pilgrim also says that the Nāgas of the Tsung-ling mountains (Hindu Kush), when evil-disposed, spit poison, winds, rain and snow, etc.[4] He notes, too, that in Udyāna a stranger was entertained for three days and was then " requested to find a place for himself." This is a Rajput custom, which is referred to by Quintus Curtius in his account of the entertainment of Alexander by Taxiles,[5] and which exists to this day.

Sung Yun, another pilgrim, entered Udyāna about A.D. 518 by way of the Kashkara (Chitrāl) valley. He records that the king of the country was then a Buddhist, who observed a vegetable diet, and that Buddhism was flourishing.[6]

This pilgrim mentions a regular system of irrigation from the rivers,[7] which indicates a considerable degree of civilization. He also describes a Nāga temple, which was served by fifty priests or more, and says that the king propitiates the

[1] " Buddhist Records," Beal, xxxi.
[2] Ib. xxx. [3] Ib. xxxi. [4] Ib. xxix.
[5] Quintus Curtius, viii. 12.
[6] " Buddhist Records," W. World, xciii. [7] Ib. xciv.

Nāga with gold and jewels and other precious offerings.[1]

Sung Yun mentions that the neighbouring kingdom of Gandhāra had been destroyed, two generations before, by Yetha invaders,[2] but these had evidently retired from the country before his visit.

A third Chinese pilgrim, Hiouen Tsiang, visited these countries about A.D. 630. He arrived by way of Bamian, Kapisa and the Kābul valley; whence he travelled through Gandhāra and Udyāna to Takshasilā. This pilgrim, like the others, found Buddhism existing in all of these countries, side by side with the worship of the Devas and the Nāgas, which were everywhere popular deities.

Describing Kapisa, or Kābul, Hiouen Tsiang says that this country is 4000 li or so in circuit; that on the north it adjoins the snowy mountains; and that on three sides it borders upon the Hindu Kush. The people he describes as "cruel and fierce." And he says: "The king is a Kshatriya by caste. He is shrewd, brave and determined, and he has brought into subjection the neighbouring countries, some ten of which he rules."[3] The king was a Buddhist, and there were about one hundred viharas and six thousand priests. There were also some ten temples of Devas. There were about one thousand heretics. There were naked

[1] "Buddhist Records," xcvi. [2] Ib. c. [3] Ib. i. 55.

ascetics, too, and some "who covered themselves with ashes, and others who made chaplets of bones, which they wore as crowns upon their heads.[1]

These are all well-known forms of Hindu asceticism.

About two hundred li from the royal city was a great snowy mountain, upon which was a lake. Here, whoever asked for rain or prayed for fine weather, had his desires fulfilled by the Nāga demi-god of the lake.[2] In old times there had been an Arhat, belonging to Gandhāra, who received the religious offerings of the Nāga king.[3] That is he acted as his priest.

The pilgrim says that a former Nāga raja of this lake was killed by another Nāga, who seized upon his possessions, and caused great mischief by raising storms. A stupa and vihara, built by Kanishka raja, were six times destroyed by the Nāga. At last Kanishka collected his army, intending to destroy the serpent chief, but he then submitted.[4]

In Lamghān, which was subject to Kapisa, there were about ten sungharamas with few followers, and there were several scores of Deva temples. In a great cavern was the abode (shrine) of the Nāga Gopāla.[5] At Hidda, a neighbouring

[1] "Buddhist Records," Beal, i. 55. [2] Ib. i. 62.
[3] Ib. i. 63. [4] Ib. i. 64. [5] Si-Yu-Ki, Beal, i. 93.

town, were many relics of Buddha, including a skull bone and an eyeball.[1]

In Gandhāra, which was then governed by an officer from Kapiśa, was the ancestral home of the king of Kābul and of so many neighbouring countries. Hiouen Tsiang, on his way back to China, was entertained by this king at the city of Udabhāndapura, or Waihand, which, as noticed by Cunningham, and more fully by Stein, was one of the capitals of the Hindu Shāhiya dynasty. The pilgrim marched with the king by way of Lamghān to Kabul.[2] This again shows that the Kshatriya king of Kābul was one of the Sāhis of the Kator or Pāla dynasty of Gandhāra.

The pilgrim describes some of the towns and villages as deserted, but others were rich and prosperous. There were many sungharamas and stupas, some of them in ruins, and many temples of the Devas. It is mentioned too that men came from every part of India to pay their vows at the temple of Bhimā Devi.[3]

This is the country which is said by Sung Yun, in A.D. 520, to have been destroyed by the Yetha two generations before. The Hindu rajas had evidently recovered possession.

Hiouen Tsiang next came to Udyāna, which has been described by the earlier pilgrims. Here

[1] Si-Yu-Ki, Beal, i. 96. [2] Hiouen Tsiang, Memoirs, 192.
[3] Si-Yu-Ki, Beal, i. 113.

he found the law of Buddha greatly respected, but Buddhism was less flourishing than formerly. There were temples of the Devas, and the Nāga demigods still ruled the elements and still presided over the lakes and fountains.

The pilgrim visited the fountain of the Nāga Apalāla,[1] which was the source of the Swat river. He visited also the stupa built by Uttara Sena, the Sākya king of Udyāna, over the relics of Buddha, whose kinsman he was.[2] Hiouen Tsiang relates the history of Uttara Sena, and of his marriage with the daughter of the Nāga raja, through whose influence he obtained the kingdom. He also says that over the head of the princess appeared the hoods of a nine-headed Nāga.[3]

After visiting Darel and some other neighbouring valleys, Hiouen Tsiang made his way to Takshasilā, which he says was then tributary to Kashmir, but had formerly been subject to Kabul.[4] Here, too, Buddhism seems to have been less flourishing than formerly. There were many sungharamas, but they were ruinous and deserted.

The pilgrim tells us that, when the people of Takshasilā wished for rain or fine weather, they went with Buddhist priests to the tank of the Nāga raja Elapatra, where, after praying, they immediately obtained their desires.[5]

[1] Hiouen Tsiang, Bael, i. 122. [2] Ib. i. 126. [3] Ib. i. 132.
[4] Hiouen Tsiang, Beal, i. 136. [5] Ib. i. 137.

The attention of the Buddhist pilgrims was, of course, directed mainly to Buddhist monuments and institutions; but their accounts of the countries through which they passed are full of interest.

From this source we learn that the kingdoms to the south of the Hindu Kush, from Kābul to the Indus, were down to the seventh century of our era still inhabited by Hindus. We learn, too, that the Buddhist religion then existed, throughout these countries, side by side with the worship of the Brāhmanical gods and of the Devas and the Nāgas. We find, too, that the Nāga demigods were everywhere popular deities, who ruled the elements, and to whom fountains, lakes and streams were sacred.

Thus it seems evident that down to the time of the early Mohammedan invasions, which took place in the middle of the seventh century—only a few years after Hiouen Tsiang's visit—the country round Kābul, and between Kābul and Kashmir was still inhabited by a Nāga-worshipping people. And there can be little doubt that these people were descendants of the serpent race of Ahi or Azi, who, in this very tract, opposed the invading Aryas. It seems, too, that the paramount rulers of this people were the Kator Sāhis of Kābul and Gandhāra.

To this dynasty, which is doubtless referred to by Abu Rihan, in a passage which has given rise to much discussion,[1] belonged Rajpāl, Anandpāl, Trilochanpāl and other less known chiefs before them, who so long and so stubbornly resisted the Mohammedan invaders.

Kābulistan must have passed through many vicissitudes during the troublous times which followed the overthrow of the great Persian empire by Alexander. It no doubt fell for a time under the sway of foreign rulers. The great mass of the population, however, must have remained Hindu. Probably too the native chiefs retained some shadow of authority, and asserted themselves when opportunity arose.

According to Chinese Buddhist records, Guna Varman, grandson of an ex-king of Kābul, arrived in China by way of Ceylon and Java in A.D. 424, and made his way to the capital of the Sung dynasty.[2]

From this it would seem that there were Hindu kings in Kābul more than two centuries before Hiouen Tsiang's arrival, in about A.D. 631, when he found a Kshatriya king upon the throne.

Kābul was the coronation city of the Pāla dynasty, and no king was considered to be properly inaugurated until he had been installed there.[3]

[1] Alberuni, Sachau, ii. 13.

[2] M. Anesaki, J.R.A.S., April, 1903, p. 369.

[3] Albiruni, Sachau, App. ii. 394; Ibn Haukal, Ouseley, 226.

We learn from Mohammedan historians that Kabul was first taken by the armies of Islām in the time of Muāwiya, about the middle of the seventh century, some twenty years or so after the visit of Hiouen Tsiang. The king, who is called by the Mussulmān historians Kābul Shah (the Sāhi of Kabul), made an appeal to the warriors of Hind. These gathered to his assistance in such numbers, that the invaders were driven out of Kābul and the neighbouring country, as far as Bost.[1]

Whether this king of Kābul was the same chief who entertained the Chinese pilgrim is uncertain; but he too must have been a Kshatriya, or the warriors of Hind would have taken little notice of his appeal.

The Mussulmān armies returned with large reinforcements, and Kābul was again taken, when the king agreed to pay tribute.

After the occupation of Kabul by the Mohammedans the chiefs of the Hindu Shahya dynasty resided chiefly at Udakabhānda. They were still powerful and held nearly the whole Panjāb. Their rule extended from Sarhind to Lamghān, and from Kashmir to Multān,[2] until their final overthrow by Mahmud in the eleventh century. During the long period of nearly four hundred

[1] Elliot, ii. 415.

[2] Ferishta, Briggs, i. 15.

years, the Kator Ṣāhis were engaged in almost continuous warfare with the Moslem invaders.

It was doubtless the genealogy of these Sāhis of Kābul which is referred to by Albiruni as having been found written on silk in the fort of Nagarkot, or Kangra.[1] This celebrated fortress was the stronghold of the Trigarta or Jalandhara family, with whom the Sāhis intermarried.[2]

So powerful were the Kator chiefs that, in the Rājatarangini, the glory of the Sāhi, amongst kings, is compared to that of the sun, amongst the stars of heaven.[3]

All the leading chiefs of Northern India sent their contingents to assist the Sāhis against the Mohammedan invaders.[4] Of these chiefs, the Chohān raja of Ajmir is expressly said to have been related to the Sāhi Jaipāl.

Some of the tribes to the south of the Hindu Kush, although now Mohammedans, are still known by the names given to them by Manu.

Wilson observed that the Kambōjas were probably represented by the Kafir tribe of Kamōj.[5] And it seems not unlikely that a remnant of the Kambōjas may have been driven into the moun-

[1] Albiruni, Sachau, ii. 11.
[2] Rajatarangini, Stein, vii. 150, 152.
[3] Ib. v. 152–155.
[4] Ferishta, Briggs, i. 18 ; i. 46. Elliot, ii. 415.
[5] Vishnu Purāna, Wilson, 374, note.

tains by some of the invaders of the country. Popular tradition says, in fact, that the Kamōj were driven out of the country of Candahār.[1] (Gandhāra).

The Kambōjas and Gandhāras appear to have been neighbours at the time described in the Mahābhārata.

The Shinas or Chinas, and their neighbours the Daradas, are described by Manu as fallen Kshatriyas.[2] They are also mentioned, in the Mahābhārata, in connexion with the Kambōjas, Kasmiras and other northern tribes.[3]

The Shinas, who are doubtless the Chinas of the Mahābhārata, and are still in some places called China or Chināl, are, like most of their neighbours, of Solar race.

A Shina song, quoted by Biddulph, runs thus:—

> "The forest serpent Suri Mahomed Khan,
> The forest serpent rouses himself.
> Beyond Shahrot he will brandish his sword,
> The forest serpent of the race of Mallika."[4]

Here the chief bears a Mohammedan name, but he is declared to be of serpent race; while Sūri is the Shina name for the Sun.

The Shinas, though now Mohammedans, retain

[1] Elphinstone, Cābul, 620. [2] Manu, Bühler, x. 43.
[3] Mahābhārata, Sabha, Dyuta, parv. xxxix.
[4] "Tribes of Hindu Kush," 87.

many of their ancient customs, which are much the same as those existing in the Himālaya. The cedar and the juniper are held sacred and are believed to afford protection from evil spirits. The seed-corn, before sowing, is purified in the smoke of the cedar.[1]

The Daradas still inhabit the left bank of the Indus. They are frequently alluded to in the Rājatarangini, and they held then, as they do now, the country between the north-western boundary of Kashmir and the Indus. The Darada chiefs, like those of Kator, were called Sāhi or Shāhi.[2]

The Daradas, although they are described in the Mahābhārata as "good and well-born Kshatriyas," had evidently, like their neighbours, come but little under Brahmanical influence, even down to the time of their conversion to Islām.

Amongst the tribes of the Hindu Kush, springs are still supposed to cause storms if any impurity be thrown into them, owing to the resentment of the Sun or of the Nāga, to whichever they may be sacred. A snow-storm, produced in this way, is said to have induced the Shāhi Jaipāl to submit to the Amir Subuktigin.[3]

In the states of Hunza and Nagar the rulers,

[1] "Tribes of Hindu Kush," 104.
[2] Rajatarangini, Stein, vii. 913.
[3] Elliott, ii. 20.

though now Mohammedans, are still believed to have power over the elements,[1] as had the Ahi of the Rig Veda and other Nāga rajas.

[1] "Tribes of Hindu Kush," 95.

CHAPTER VI

It seems probable that Takha, or Katha, was not a tribal name, but an appellation bestowed upon several tribes.

The Takhas are not mentioned, either by that name or by any of its present-day variants, amongst the people engaged in the wars of the Mahābhārata; nor are any of these called Nāgas. People called Bāhikas, Bāhlikas, or Vāhlikas, however, are frequently noticed, and these are said, by Hemachandra, to have been also called Takhas.[1]

The Bāhikas, or Bāhlikas, were allies of the Kauravas in the great war. They were evidently a powerful people, who held a great extent of country. The territories they occupied seem to have corresponded with the dominions assigned to the Nāga rajas, and with the Takhia kingdom of later times.

The term Bāhika, or Bāhlika, was evidently not a tribal name, and its origin is uncertain. Some have supposed that these people must have been invaders from Balkh. They were not,

[1] Lassen, Pentap. Ind., 21.

however, recent invaders, even at that remote period. Although they are not mentioned in the Rig Veda, as noted by Kern, they are referred to in the Atharva Veda,[1] and they are also mentioned by Panini as a people established in India, who had a dialect differing somewhat from that of their neighbours.[2] They were settled in the Panjāb before the time of the Ramāyana, as the messengers sent by Dasarath, to recall Bhārata from Kekāya, passed through Panchāla, Kurujangala, and through the midst of Vāhlika.[3]

Bāhlika, or Vāhlika, appears to have been a general term applied to a number of tribes or clans, of Solar race, who were more or less closely related to each other. These are mentioned in connection with, and probably included, the Prasthalas, Madras, Gandhāras, Ārattas, Khasas, Vasatis, Sindhus and Sauviras.[4] The Bāhlikas are described as dwelling in the countries through which flow the rivers Satadru (Sutlej), Vipasa (Beās), Irāvati (Rāvi), Chandra-bāgha (Chināb), Vitasta (Jhelam), and Sindhu (Indus)[5]; that is to say, in the Panjāb, Sind, and Rājputana. In

[1] Muir, O.S.T. ii. 446.
[2] Ib. 354 (note).
[3] Ramāyana, Cal. ed., II. liii. 107.
[4] Mahābhārata, Karna parva., xliv.
[5] Ib.

those days the Sutlej flowed much further south than it does at present.[1]

These people were ruled by numerous chiefs, who were referred to as the hundred kings of Bāhlika.

At the time of the great war the paramount ruler of the Bāhlikas was Salya, a grandson of Somadatta, or Vāhlika, a Bhārata chief who had succeeded to the throne of the Bhālika raja, his maternal grandfather.[2] Salya and other Bhālika chiefs were present at the swayambara, or choice of a husband, of Rukmini, when she was carried off by Krishna.[3]

Although the Bāhlikas, or Takhas, were "good and well-born Kshatriyas,"[4] and intermarried with the Bhāratas, they were evidently unregenerate, and had not yet adopted Aryan customs. This is confirmed, as we shall soon see, by the practices ascribed to them.

The Madras were one of the most important tribes of the Bāhlikas. Sākala, the capital of the Bāhlika raja, was a city of the Madras.[5] In the Kathā Sarit Sagara the Madras are said to

[1] J.R.A.S., Jan., 1893.

[2] Mahābhārata, Adi, Sambhava, p. cxxvi. Ib. Udyoga, Bhagavatyana, p. cxlviii.

[3] Harivansa, Langlois, cxx. 493.

[4] Mahābhārata, Sabha, Dyuta, p. xxxix.

[5] Ib. Sabha, Digvijaya, p. xxxii.

be Dānavas,[1] and all these tribes were doubtless of Asura descent.

The Kurus and Panchālas, who had evidently come under Brahmanical influence, are said to be "conversant with the truths of religion"; but not so the Madrakas and the other people of the "Five Rivers."[2]

Many of the customs, ascribed to the Bāhlikas were certainly much opposed to the rules laid down by Brahmanical law-givers. Possibly some of the improprieties may have been exaggerated, but not a few of them still exist amongst the descendants of these people.

The Madras, as one of their greatest offences are said to have had Kshatriyas for their priests.[3] This, it may be noted, confirms other passages, showing that the Bāhlikas were Kshatriyas, and that they belonged to no servile caste, and to no tribe of outside barbarians. We find, however, that they had not adopted a fixed caste system, but that there were Brāhmans and Kshatriyas in the same family.[4]

These people are described as eating out of wooden and earthen vessels, and as drinking the milk of sheep and of camels,[5] which some of them do to this day. It is said, too, that the Jartika

[1] Kathā Sarit Sagara, Tawney, i. 416.
[2] Mahābhārata, Karna, p. xlv.
[3] Ib. [4] Ib. [5] Ib. p. xliv.

clan of Bāhikas and the people of Sākala ate beef with garlic,[1] and that all the tribes drank strong liquors. A slaughter-ground for cattle, and a place for storing intoxicating drink, are said to mark the entrance to the dwellings of the Vāhika chiefs.[2] The women, too, are accused of drinking and dancing in public, and otherwise misconducting themselves.[3] Some of these heterodox practices, however, prevailed amongst the orthodox Yādavas and Bhāratas at Dwārakā and Indraprastha. We find that the Yādava women at Dwārakā danced and sang at festivals, and that the rishi Nārada played for them on the vina.[4] Again, when Krishna and Arjuna went, with their families and friends, to a fête on the banks of the Yamunā, the ladies, amongst whom were Draupadi and Subhadrā, drank wine; some of them, too, danced and sang; and some even became unsteady in their gait.[5] All these practices, so much opposed to the rules laid down by Hindu law-givers, were doubtless Asura customs, which had not yet yielded to Brahmanical influence.

For Kshatriyas to act as priests at both Deva and Nāga temples is, as already noticed, still common in the Himālaya. This custom, how-

[1] Mahābhārata, Karna, p. xliv. [2] Ib.
[3] Ib. xliv. [4] Harivansa, Langlois, II. cxlvi. 101.
[5] Mahābhārata, Adi, Khāndavadaha, p. ccxxiv.

ever, is not unknown to the Rajputs of the plains. Colonel Tod tells us that the Ranas of Mewar, when they visit the temple of Siva, supersede the priest and perform the ceremonies.[1] This practice occurs at other temples. We are told in the Ras Mala that, at the shrine of Amba Bhowanie Mata, the tutelary deity of the Prāmāras, the Rana himself offers sacrifice, fans the idol with a chāori, and takes the offerings.[2] At Rajim, in Kosala, too, are some ancient temples sacred to Vishnu, and of one of the oldest of these the pujaries are Bais Rajputs.[3] Here we have the Asura custom of Kshatriya priests, as it existed amongst the Bāhlikas, still surviving amongst orthodox Hindus.

It is said that when Vishnu, in the Dwarf Avatara, took away the dominions of the Daitya chief Bali, with the exception of Pātala, the Asura king was allowed to retain six privileges. Of these, one was that he should make a sraddha without Brāhmans, and another was that he should make an offering without a priest.[4] This seems to point to a religious compact, or "Concordat," between the Āryas and the Asuras. At the time described in the Mahābhārata, many Kshatriya tribes were still unregenerate. The

[1] "Annals of Rajasthan," i. 446.

[2] Ras Mala, 323. [3] Ind. Arch. Reports, vii. 9.

[4] Harivansa, ii. 490.

Prasthalas or Trigarttas, Madras, Gandhāras, Arattas, Khasas, Vasatis, Sindhus, and Sauviras are said to be all equally wicked;[1] and some of the others were not much better. The Madras received a price for their daughters on marriage, which is contrary to Brahmanical precept. We find, however, that Bhishma, the Bhārata chief, conformed to this practice when he sought to obtain Madri as a wife for Pāndu. And he paid "much gold," besides jewels, to Salya, the elder brother of the princess, who, as head of the family, gave her away.

We have just seen that amongst the evil customs assigned to the Bāhlikas is the use of wooden and earthen vessels to contain food. The descendants of these people seem still to have a prejudice against the brass vessels used by all orthodox Hindus, and a preference for those of wood or earthenware. Owing to the scarcity of suitable wood in the Panjāb plains, earthen vessels are generally seen. These are usually broken after being used by a stranger. Where timber is plentiful, as in the Hindu Kush or Himālaya, wooden vessels are very common. These are usually of an oval shape and "deep-bellied," as described in the Mahābhārata.

[1] Mahābhārata, Karna, p. xliv.
[2] Mahābhārata, Adi, Sambhava, p. cxiii.
[3] Ib. Karna, p. xliv.

As we have already seen, the Madras were Bāhlikas, or Takhas. Sākala, therefore, the capital of Salya the Bāhlika raja, was a Takha city. Sākala was on the Āpaga, or Aik river,[1] and was the Sangala of the Greeks. This city was, at the time of Alexander's invasion in the fourth century B.C., a fortress of the Kāthias,[2] who, as already noted, were included amongst the Takhas. When visited by the Chinese pilgrim, Hiouen Tsiang, in the seventh century A.D., Sākala was in ruins, but the surrounding country still formed part of the kingdom of Takha, or Takhia.[3] And it did so, at the time of the Arab invasion of Sind, in the eighth century.[4] Moreover, the Kāthia tribe to this day hold lands round their ancient stronghold.

The descendants of the Bāhikas, or Bāhlikas, who still live amongst "the forests of Pilu and Karira," on the banks of the "Five Rivers," as their forefathers did in the time of Salya,[5] are now Mohammedans; but they retain many of the customs ascribed to their ancestors, in the Mahābhārata, and by the chroniclers of Alexander's invasion. They are divided into numerous

[1] Mahābhārata, Karna, p. xliv.
[2] Arrian Expedio. Alex. v. xxii.
[3] Hiouen Tsiang, Beal, I. iv. 165, 166.
[4] Elliot, i. 178.
[5] Mahābhārata, Karna, p. xliv.

tribes or clans, of which the Kāthias are amongst the most powerful.

These people, notwithstanding their conversion to Islām, are proud of their Kshatriya descent; but, of course, they no longer worship the Nāga demi-gods. They still retain the handsome features and fine physique by which the Greeks were so much impressed.[1] Their sacred groves, once the abode of the gods, are still religiously preserved. In them no tree is felled, nor even a branch broken. These are now used as burial-places, and bodies are brought from long distances to be laid in them.

Women, amongst these people, are still allowed much more freedom than is generally the case in India. They are not secluded; the daughters, like the heroines of the Mahābhārata, are married as grown-up young women; and infant marriage is unknown. The men allow their hair and beards to grow, as described by the Greek writers; and the youths go bareheaded till they reach manhood, when the father ties a scanty pagri, or turban, (the fillet of Strabo [2]), round his son's head. Until recently this ceremony was not performed till the youth had shown his prowess, by killing an enemy, or by lifting cattle. I once heard a village patriarch acknowledge that this was the custom of his people, and he added,

[1] Quintus Curtius, ix. 149. [2] Strabo, Geog. XV. i. 71.

regretfully, that it had become very difficult to carry it out. This was said *à propos* of his grandson, who stood by, smiling and bareheaded. No doubt the youth won his turban not long after. In the early days of British rule, in the Panjāb, almost the only crimes amongst these people were cattle-stealing and the affrays resulting from it. These latter often ended fatally to some of those engaged.

In most villages were men called "Kōjis," who could follow the footmarks of men or cattle for almost any distance, and whose services were in frequent demand.

When stolen cattle were traced to a village, and there seemed no hope of evading punishment, it was not uncommon for some of the old men to give themselves up, in order to screen the young ones who were the real criminals. This was probably a survival from the good old times, when the necessity for keeping up the fighting strength of the tribe was urgent.

These people are, with their relatives the Sikhs, the finest race in India.

Some of the Kāthias and other descendants of the Bāhlikas, as well as branches of other Kshatriya tribes, are called Jats. The origin of the Jats has been much discussed. Some authorities have considered them to be descendants of invading Scythian hordes. There can be no doubt, however, that, whatever its origin, the term Jat has long been applied to the descendants of those Kshatriyas who clung to their ancient customs; and to branches of Rajput tribes who, in consequence of irregular practices, have been cast off by their more orthodox relatives.

Nearly every Rajput tribe has Jat branches. Thus, the Bhattis of Jessalmer, who are Rajputs of the Lunar line, apply the term Jat, in their genealogical lists, to those of their own tribe who have married beneath them, have adopted unorthodox practices,[1] or have become converts to Islām.[2]

In the Panjāb the Kāthias, Khurrals, Johyas, and other tribes, are each divided into Rajputs and Jats.[3] In other parts of India the same conditions occur, and Jat clans are found of undoubted Rajput descent. Sir H. Elliot mentions a tribe of Jats who are descended, in the direct line, from Rai Pirthiraj Chohān.[4]

It has been pointed out by M. Vivien de St. Martin that Jartika, the name given in the Mahābhārata to one branch of the Bāhlikas, is a Sanskritized form of the term Jat.[5] This shows

[1] "Annals of Rajasthan," ii. 249.

[2] Ib. i. 106, 108.

[3] Panjāb Gazetteer, Montgomery, 60; "Annals of Rajasthan," ii. 181.

[4] Elliot, Sup. Glossary, 147.

[5] Étude sur la Géog. de l'Inde (1860), 251.

that there were Jats on the banks of the "Five Rivers" at the time of the great war, and goes far to confirm the view that Rajputs and Jats are of the same stock, the difference between them being one of orthodoxy only.

The Kāthis, or Kāthias, of Kāthiawar, are a branch of the Kāthias of the Panjāb. According to the tribal traditions, this branch of the Kāthias was settled in the country now called Bikanir,[1] and from thence moved to the Indus valley. Later they passed on to Kāthiawar, where they arrived in the thirteenth century.[2] Other portions of the tribe wandered in other directions, and of these some seem to have found their way to the Ganges valley. It is probable that this migration was caused by the great change in the course of the Sutlej, which occurred about that time.[3] This river then forsook its ancient channel, now called the "Hakra," and joined the Beas. This change of course left without water a vast tract of hitherto fertile land, with many important towns and great numbers of villages. Tradition says that, in consequence of this, thousands of men and cattle died of drought and famine, and that most of the survivors took refuge in the Indus

[1] Panjāb Gazetteer, Montgomery, 64, 65.

[2] Ras Mala, ii. 269.

[3] J.R.A.S., Jan., 1893.

valley. The country on the banks of this old bed of the Sutlej is now a desert.

The Kāthis of Kāthiawar are more or less orthodox Hindus, but they still venerate the sun and the serpent. Shrines sacred to Vāsuki and other Nāga demi-gods are numerous amongst them,[1] and Colonel Tod tells us that they are of the race of Takshaka.[2] In attesting important legal documents, they call to witness "the holy sun."

The Kāthis claim to have been allies of the Kauravas in the great war of the Mahābhārata.[3] As already mentioned, they were a branch of the Kāthias. An inscription from Rāmchandrapur, near Būndi in Rajputana, quoted by Colonel Tod, says that the warrior Takhya, who formed the garland (of skulls) on the neck of Mahādeo, was of the Catti (Kāthi) tribe.[4] Closely connected with the Kāthis, and apparently of the same stock,[5] are the Vāhlas, or Bāhlas, or Bāhilkas, who are said to have been lords of Arore in the Indus valley, and whose chiefs were addressed by the bards as "Tatha Multān ka rai," or kings of Tatha and Multān.[6] This title is also given to the Kāthis,[7] and the term Kāthiani bai, or

[1] Ind. Ant., July, 1875, 193.
[2] "Annals of Rajasthan," i. 702.
[3] Ind. Antiq., iv. 321.
[4] "Annals of Rajasthan," i. 112.
[5] Ras Mala, i. 296.
[6] "Annals of Rajasthan," i. 112.
[7] Tod, Western India, 207.

Kāthia lady, is sometimes applied to ladies of Vāhla family.[1] Bālas and Kāthis are probably branches of the same people.

The name Vāhla, or Bāla, recalls that of the great Asura Bali of Pātala, who also ruled from the mouth of the Indus to Multān. It seems at least possible that the Bālika rais, who in later times held the same tract of country, may have been descendants of the Daitya king.

We have seen, from the Mahābhārata, that the Bāhlikas, or Takhas, occupied the country on the banks of the Indus at a very early period.[2] And the inscription upon the iron pillar at Delhi, which is supposed to have been erected by Chandra Gupta II, about A.D. 415, says that this ancient monument was erected in celebration of a victory over the Vāhlikas of Sindhu.[3] The Indus valley, therefore, down to the time when this pillar was first erected, was still held by Bāhlika chiefs. Moreover, as we have already seen, Multān and the neighbouring country formed a part of the kingdom of Takhya at the time of Hiouen Tsiang's visit in the seventh century.

Down to this period, therefore, the descendants of the Nāga rajas still ruled in the Indus valley.

[1] Kathiawar Gazetteer, 130.

[2] Mahābhārata, Karna, p. xliv.

[3] J.A.S. Bengal, 1839, 629, 631; Delhi Gazetteer, 186; V. Smith, J.R.A.S., Jan., 1897, p. 10.

More than one of these Kshatriya tribes appear to have been known by several different names. Some of these may, as already noted, have been mere epithets applied to them by their bards or by their neighbours, while others were perhaps adopted by offshoots from the main stem.

The Takhas, or Kathas, as we have seen, were not called by those names in the epic poems, but were known as Bāhlikas. The powerful Puārs, or Pramāras, also, were not mentioned under either of these names in the Mahābhārata.

The dominions of the Puārs extended from the Indus to the Jumna, and even beyond. And it appears probable that the Indian rajas, who opposed the Greeks, and were called Porus by the chroniclers of Alexander's expedition, and Phūr by Ferishta and other historians, belonged to this powerful tribe.

By the historians of Alexander two contemporary chiefs were called Porus, and these were related to each other. It would seem, therefore, that this was a tribal, or racial, and not a personal name.

Ferishta says, too, that Phūr was raja of Kathēr, or Kamāon,[1] which, according to the bards, was included in the Puār dominions.[2]

Mr. Grierson has lately drawn attentionto the

[1] Ferishta, Briggs, lxxiii.
[2] "Annals of Rajasthan," i. 92.

close relationship between the dialects of Rājasthan and those of the Himālaya.[1]

The population of Magadha and the neighbouring country, in which Buddha spent the greater part of his life, was then, and in later times, largely made up of Nāga tribes.

According to the Vishnu Purāna, Vidmisara, or Bimbisaro, who reigned at Rajagriha, and was a friend of Buddha, was a great-great-grandson of Sisunāga,[2] King of Magadha.

The great Asoka, grandson of Chandragupta Morya, seems to have worshipped the Nāga even after his conversion to Buddhism.

We are told that when Asoka heard that Mahākālo, the Nāga raja, had seen the last four Buddhas, he sent for him, or rather for the living serpent which represented him. When the Nāga arrived, Asoka placed him "on the royal throne, under the white canopy of dominion," and making many flower offerings, requested to be shown the appearance of Buddha. This request, we are told, was granted.[3]

In the time of Asoka, Nāga rajas were numerous and powerful.

We find that when this king, wishing to divide the relics of Buddha amongst the new stupas

[1] J.R.A.S., Oct., 1901.

[2] Vishnu Purāna, IV. xxiv. 466.

[3] Mahawanso, v. 27; Burnouf, Intro. Hist. Budd. Ind., 332.

NĀG SULA
(SACRED TO PADAM NĀG)
KAMAON.

which he had built, went with an army to remove the relics from the old stupa at Ramāgrama, the Nāgas refused to allow him to do so. And Asoka, powerful as he was, did not persist.[1]

This stupa is said to have been afterwards carried away by the river. The relics, however, were rescued by the Nāga people, who took them to Majerika, on the Kistna river, where the Nāga raja, who ruled that country, built a very magnificent stupa over them.[2]

In the Vishnu Purāna it is said that nine Nāgas will reign in Padmavati, Kantipura, and Matharā.[3] It has been shown by Sir A. Cunningham that these serpent chiefs, whose names he gives from their coins, held most of the country between the Jumna and the Narbada; and that they ruled, as independent princes, during the first two centuries of the Christian era.[4]

According to the inscription upon the Allahabad pillar, most of the Nāga chiefs of any importance, who remained in his time, seem to have been overthrown by Samudra Gupta.

The Nāga people disappear from history about the time of the downfall of the Buddhist religion. Probably the Brahmanic revival was fatal to both, and the Nāgas, like the Buddhists, were induced, or compelled, to adopt orthodox Hinduism.

[1] Burnouf, Intro. Hist. Budd. Ind., 332.
[2] Anct. Geog. Ind., 534, 535. [3] Vishnu Purāna, IV. xxiv. 479.
[4] Ind. Arch. Reports, ii. 308.

CHAPTER VII

THE earliest civilization of southern India is generally ascribed to the Dravidians. And most authorities consider that this people came from northern India. It has been supposed that they were displaced by the invading Āryas.

Dr. Caldwell, a very eminent authority, asks: "Were the Dravidians identical with the Dasyus, by whom the progress of the Aryans was disputed, and who were finally subdued and incorporated with the Aryan race, as their serfs and dependants?"[1] Here, as elsewhere, it is assumed that the Āryas were conquerors, who reduced the Asuras to slavery. It has already been shown, however, in these pages, that this was not the case. We have seen that there was a fusion of the two peoples. We have also seen that, whatever may have been the fate of the aborigines, the Asuras were not subdued by the Āryas, and never became their serfs or dependants, but were gradually converted to Aryan usages.

Dr. Caldwell himself says: "Neither the

[1] Grammar of Drav. Languages, Intro., 107.

subjugation of the Dravidians by the Aryans, nor the expulsion from northern India of the southern Dravidians by the Aryans, is recognized by any Sanscrit authority or any Dravidian tradition."[1] But although the Asuras or Dravidians had neither been subjugated nor expelled from northern India, they had, in very early times, established colonies in the south; as we have seen in the case of the Nāgas, sons of Kadru, and of Lavana before them. Some of these colonies were in the very positions occupied by the Dravidian kingdoms; and there can be little doubt that Asura colonists were the founders of those kingdoms.

These Dravidian colonies, some of which may have been established before the Āryas entered India, appear to have been founded by expeditions sent, some by sea, from Pātala and other ports, and some by land.

Ancient legends refer to conflicts between the Hindu colonists of later times, said to have been led by Parasu Rāma, and the Nāgas from Pātala, whom they found in possession of the country.[2]

Inscriptions, too, of the tenth and eleventh centuries, show that several of the chiefs of south-western India claimed to have been born in the

[1] Grammar of Drav. Languages, Intro., 108.

[2] V. Nāgam Ayar, Travancore Census Report (1891), 384.

race of the Nāgas ; to have held the Nāga dhwaja, or serpent banner ; and to have had the hereditary title of "supreme lord of Bhōgavati."[1] They thus claimed direct descent from the Nāga rajas of Pātala.

A part of the country of Kanara was called in inscriptions Nāgarakhanda, or the territory of the Nāga people.[2]

The earliest settlements in Ceylon were founded by the same people, though they appear to have been afterwards partially expelled by invaders from India.

We have already seen that the great Rāvana, the foe of Rāma, was a Nāga chief, whose family lived in Pātala. His kingdom was, doubtless, one of the Nāga colonies.

The existence of powerful chiefs of serpent race in Ceylon, before the time of Buddha, is referred to by Buddhist authorities.[3]

Although their colonies were numerous and extensive, there does not appear to have been any general migration southwards of the Asura people. They never abandoned their possessions in northern India ; and in the new territories, even where dynasties were established, the greater

[1] Fleet, Bombay Gazetteer, I. ii. 576–7.

[2] Ib. 281 (note).

[3] Mahāwanso, Turnour, i. 5 ; i. 7, 209. Dipavansa, xx. 21–24.

part of the population seems to have remained of Nishāda or aboriginal race, as in the kingdom of the Nāga raja Dhūmavarna, which has been already referred to. The invaders however appear to have been able, owing to their superior civilization, to impress to a great extent, upon the rude aboriginal people, their social customs, their religion, and their language. The Dravidian colonists, too, seem to have intermixed to some extent with the surrounding population, which would be sufficient to account for the caste of Sudra having been assigned to their descendants. This may also help to explain the existence of Dravidian dialects and customs amongst people, as the Gonds and others, whose appearance would seem to indicate aboriginal descent, rather than any relationship to the inhabitants of the Indus valley or Panjāb.

Long after the time of these early colonists, when the Devas and Asuras had become one people, and the Saiva and Vaishnava forms of Hinduism had become established in northern India, the worship of the Brahmanical deities was introduced in the south. The people, however, seem to have retained much of their ancient religion and mode of life. Hence the widespread veneration for the Nāga demi-gods, the great number of unorthodox deities, with their equally unorthodox rites, and the many customs, not recognized by Brahmanical law-givers, which still survive.

Most of these forms of religion and many of these customs still exist, in parts of northern India, amongst people who are apparently descendants of the Nāgas or Asuras.

The worship of the Nāga or hooded serpent is general amongst the Dravidian people of the south. Rudely sculptured representations of the serpent or of the Nāga demi-gods, to which offerings are regularly made, are to be found under nearly every large tree. Here, as in the north, it is the Nāga or Cobra, here called Chera, which is held sacred, is a welcome visitor, and must not be killed. Here, too, as in the Himālaya, it is as the totem of their Nāga forefathers that the Nulla Paumbhu, or good snake, is venerated.

To the Nāga demi-gods, as ancestors, divine honours are paid. And amongst these ancestors, of the Dravidians, are the same Nāga rajas who are worshipped, also as ancestors, by the descendants of the Asuras in the north of India. As already mentioned, the offerings made to living serpents, as well as to their sculptured representatives, consist of milk, flour, fruit, and grain, which are not the usual food of snakes, but are the food of men. Flowers and lights are also offered, as to ancestors. We find, too, that should a cobra be killed, it is burned as if it were a human body; and it is even provided with a winding-sheet.[1]

Amongst the Dravidians, the Nāga demi-gods are usually worshipped in Kavūs or groves, which, like the sacred groves near so many Panjāb villages, are left untouched by axe or spade.[2]

One of these Kāvūs occupies the south-west corner of the enclosure round each Nair house. Sometimes these groves are very extensive, and many of the temples are richly endowed. One of the most famous temples in Travancore is that of the Nāga raja at Nagarcoil.[3]

A Nāga Kavū, near Travancore, is the property of a family whose ancestors, according to ancient tradition, were amongst the Nāgas spared when the Khāndava forest, in the Panjāb, was burned by the confederate tribes led by Krishna and Arjuna.[4]

Every male member of this family bears the name of Vāsuki,[5] the raja of Pātala and the deified hero of the Nāga people of northern India.

The members of this household are priests of the temple, and in the solemn procession, which

[1] Sri Kantellar, Ind. Ant., July, 1892; Panjāb N. and Q., ii. 555.

[2] Travancore Census Report, 1894, 354.

[3] Ib. 359.

[4] Mahābhārata, Adi, Khāndava-daha, p. ccxxix.

[5] Travancore Census Report, 1891, 355.

circumambulates the shrine at the festivals held in honour of the Nāga raja, the image of the serpent-god is carried by the eldest female member of the family, who is required to remain celibate.[1] Besides the groves and temples sacred to the Nāga demi-gods there are, as in northern India, groves and temples dedicated to Devas.

The language used in the services, at all these unorthodox shrines, is the local Dravidian dialect. In the Brahmanical temples, on the other hand, the worship of the orthodox deities is conducted in Sanscrit.[2]

There are also other divinities, both male and female, some of which are probably of aboriginal descent.

It is impossible not to recognize, in the so-called demon-worship of the Dravidian people, as described by Dr. Caldwell[3] and others, a more debased form of the ancestor-worship of northern India and of other countries. Some of the ritual, and possibly some of the deities, may have been borrowed from the aboriginal tribes, but the main features of the ceremonial are identical with the forms used in the worship of the Devas and Nāgas in the Himālaya. Some of the deities, too, are the same. Then, the sacred groves, the

[1] Travancore Census Report, 1891, 356.
[2] Ib. 521, 575.
[3] Grammar of Drav. Languages, 580.

temples being vested in the village communities, free from Brahmanic control, the non-Brahmanic priests, the inspired prophets, the religious dances, the circumambulation of the temples, the use of flagellation, and the ceremonial attending the erection of the Dhwaja or standard of the deity, are all common to the ancient, but no longer orthodox, Hinduism of northern India, and to the unorthodox Dravidian religion of the south.

Another link between the descendants of Asuras in the north of India, and the Dravidians of the south, is the institution of dancing-girls attached to the temples.

These represent the Apsarases or celestial nymphs, whose charms, as we learn from the epic poems and Purānas, so often, in former days, interfered with the austerities of holy men.

We find from the Mahābhārata that the Kshatriya princes of northern India frequently intermarried with the ruling Dravidian families. Thus two of the early Bhārata chiefs, Akrodhana and Tangsu, married princesses of Kalinga;[1] and Arjuna married the daughter of the king of the Pāndyas.

In later times, amongst other instances, Ranaditya, raja of Kashmir, married the daughter of Ratisena, raja of Chola.[2] This, according to the

[1] Mahābhārata, Adi, Sambhava, parva., xcv.

[2] Rātajarangini, iii. 436.

Rājatarangini, was about A.D. 300, so that in times when Brahmanical influence had become paramount, and the caste system was in full force, the ruling chiefs of the Dravidian kingdoms were recognized as of Kshatriya descent by the royal families of northern India. We have it, however, on the authority of Manu, that the Drāvidas were of Kshatriya origin. He mentions them amongst those Kshatriyas who had sunk to the condition of Sudras, through the omission of sacred rites and the neglect of Brāhmans.[1] This, of course, refers only to the ruling families and military caste. The greater part of the population must have been of aboriginal descent.

We further learn from Manu that the Drāvidas, with the Mallas, the Lichavis, the Kasas, and others, are descended from Vratya Kshatriyas.[2] The Mallas, the Lichavis, and the Kasas, although Kshatriyas, were Nāga-worshipping tribes of Solar race, who still retained the customs and religion of their Asura forefathers, and evidently, in the eyes of Manu, the Drāvidas were the same.

Karna, in his altercation with Salya, as given in the Mahābhārata, classes the Karashkaras, the Mahishākas, the Kalingas, the Keralas, the Karkotakas, and the Virakas, with the Bāhikas of

[1] Manu, Bühler, x. 43–44.
[2] Ib. x. 22.

northern India.[1] There is further evidence, however, that the serpent-worshippers of the south of India were very closely related to those of the north.

The Dravidian people have been divided, from ancient times, into Chēras, Chōlas and Pāndyas.

Chēra, or Sēra (in old Tamil Sārai) is the Dravidian equivalent for Nāga; Chēra-mandala, therefore, has the same meaning as Nāga–mandala, Nāga-dwipa, or the Nāga country. This seems to point distinctly to the Asura origin of the Dravidians of the south. But in addition to this there still exists, widely spread over the Ganges valley, a people who call themselves Chērūs or Seoris, and who claim descent from the serpent-gods.[2] The Chērūs are of very ancient race; they are believed to have once held a great portion of the valley of the Ganges, which, as we have already seen, was occupied in very early times by Nāga tribes. The Chērūs appear to have been gradually ousted from their lands, during the troublous times of the Mohammedan invasions, and they are now poor and almost landless. There can be little doubt that these people are the kinsmen of the Dravidian Chēras.

The Chērūs have several peculiar customs, and amongst them one which seems to connect them

[1] Mahābhārata, Karna, parva., xliv.

[2] Elliot, Sup. Glossary N.W.P., 135, 136.

with the Lichavis, as well as with the Newars of Nepāl. This is the election of a raja for every five or six houses, and his investiture, in due form, with the tilak or royal frontal mark.[1] Both Lichavis and Newars had many customs in common with the Dravidians of the south. Each venerated the serpent, Karkotaka Nāga being to Nepal what Nīla Nāga was to Kashmir. A Nāga, too, was the tutelary deity of Vaisāli, the Lichavi capital.

The marital relations of Newars and Lichavis closely resembled those of the Tamil people, and go far to show a common origin.

Property amongst the Newars descended in the female line, as it once did amongst the Ārattas, Bāhikas or Takhas of the Panjāb, whose sisters' sons, and not their own, were their heirs.[2] This is still a Dravidian custom. In short, a recent Dravidian writer, Mr. Balkrishna Nair, says that his people "appear to be, in nearly every particular, the kinsfolk of the Newars."[3]

Besides all this, however, there are other links connecting the Nāga people of the south with those of the north of India. In an inscription, discovered by Colonel Tod at Kanswah near the river Chambal, a raja, called Salindra, "of the race

[1] Sherring Races of N.W.P., 376, 377.
[2] Mahābhārata, Karna, p. xlv.
[3] Calcutta Review, July, 1896.

PEOPLE OF SARĀJ, BEAS VALLEY.

of Sārya, a tribe-renowned amongst the tribes of the mighty," is said to be ruler of Takhya.[1]

This was evidently the Takhya or Takha kingdom of the Panjāb, which was visited by Hiouen Tsiang,[2] and which has been already referred to. It seems, therefore, that the Nāga people of Takhya were known also by the name of Sārya.

Again, in the outer Himālaya, between the Sutlej and Beas valleys, is a tract of country called Sārāj, or Seorāj. In this district the Nāga demi-gods are the chief deities worshipped.

There is another Seorāj in the upper Chināb valley, and this too is occupied by a Nāga-worshipping people.

The name Sārāj, or Seorāj, appears to be the same as the Sārya of Colonel Tod's inscription, and as Seori, which is the alternative name of the Chērūs of the Ganges valley. It also seems to be identical with Sārai, which, as we have already seen, is the old Tamil name for the Chēra or Nāga. Apparently, therefore, the Sāryas of Takhya, the Sārāj people of the Sutlej valley, the Seoris or Chērūs of the valley of the Ganges, and the Chēras, Sēras, or Keralas of southern India, are but different branches of the same Nāga-worshipping people.

[1] "Annals of Rājasthan," i. 795.
[2] Hiouen Tsiang, Beal, i. 165.

It may be noted, too, that in some of the Himālayan dialects, Kira or Kiri means a serpent. This name, from which was perhaps derived the term Kirāta so often applied to the people of the Himālaya, is found in the Rājatarangini, where it is applied to a people in or near Kashmir. The Kiras are mentioned by Varaha Mihira, and in a copper plate published by Prof. Kielhorn ?[1]

An inscription at the Baijnath temple in the Kangra valley gives Kiragrama as the then name of the place.[2] This, in the local dialect, would mean the village of serpents. The Nāga is still a popular deity at Baijnath, and throughout the neighbouring country. The term Kira is thus an equivalent for Nāga, and it can scarcely be doubted that the serpent-worshipping Kiras of the Himālaya were closely related to the Dravidian Kēras, Chēras, or Kēralas of the south.

Similarity of name is not always to be trusted, but here we have something more. These people, whose designation is thus apparently the same, are all of Solar race; they all venerate the hooded serpent; and they all worship, as ancestors, the Nāga demi-gods.

From the foregoing it would seem tolerably certain that the Dravidians, of southern India,

[1] Rājatarangini, Stein, viii. 27, 67.
Rapson, J.R.A.S., July, 1900, 533.

[2] J.R.A.S., Jan., 1903, p. 37.

SCULPTURES AT RUINED TEMPLE, LALLA, KANGRA VALLEY.

were of the same stock as the Nāgas or Asuras of the north.

The only question remaining is that of speech. The language of the southern Dravidians differs from that of the people of northern India. It should be remembered, however, by those who may object on linguistic grounds to the common origin of the Nāgas and the Dravidians, that the Asuras being apparently of Turanian origin, their language would be a Turanian tongue.

Sir W. Jones long ago found a "Tartarian or Chaldee element" in the colloquial dialects of northern India. Later authorities, too, have considered these dialects to have Scythian affinities. Dr. Caldwell, however, goes further, and says: "Seeing that the northern vernaculars possess, with the words of the Sanscrit, a grammatical structure, which in the main appears to be Scythian, it seems more correct to represent those languages as having a Scythian basis with a large and almost overwhelming Sanscrit addition, than as having a Sanscrit basis with a small admixture of a Scythian element."[1]

There can be little doubt, from what we have already seen, that from the language of the Asuras, mainly, came the corrupting influences by which were formed the various Prakrits. And it was probably the linguistic changes, occurring during

[1] Gram. Drav. Lang. Intro., 58.

the gradual fusion of the Āryas and Dasyus, which created the necessity for so many grammarians.

It should be borne in mind, also, that the Asuras appear to have sent out their earlier colonies before their fusion with the Āryas. At that time their language could have come but little under the influence of Sanscrit. The Prakrits, on the other hand, were formed at a later period, when the two peoples had become more or less welded together. Hence, it is to be expected that the Prakrits should have a closer affinity with Sanscrit than the Dravidian languages of southern India; and that the latter should retain a more intimate connection, than the Prakrits, with Scythian or Turanian tongues.

It is evident that the old Sanscrit grammarians considered the language of the Dravidian countries to be connected with the vernaculars of northern India; and that, in their opinion, it was especially related to the speech of those people who, as we have seen, were apparently descendants of the Asura tribes. Thus, in the "Shadbasha Chandrika," Lakshmidhara says that the Paisāchi language is spoken in the Paisāchi countries of Pāndya, Kekaya, Vāhlika, Sahya, Nepāla, Kuntala, Sudesha, Bhota, Gandhāra, Haiva, and Kanōjana; and that these are the Paisāchi countries.[1] Of all

[1] Muir, O.S.T., ii. 49.

the vernacular dialects, the Paisāchi is said to have contained the smallest infusion of Sanscrit.[1]

That the Asuras originally spoke a language which differed from that of the Āryas seems evident. Several passages are quoted by Professor Muir, from the Rig Veda, in which the word "mridavach" is applied to the speech of the Asuras (R. V. i. 74, 2; v. vi. 3; v. vii. 6). Of these passages, Professor Muir observes: "The word mridavach, which I have translated 'injuriously speaking,' is explained by Sāyana as meaning one whose organs of speech are destroyed."[2] The original meaning of the expression was, doubtless, that the language of the Asuras was more or less unintelligible to the Āryas. The same explanation will apply to another passage in the Rig Veda, where it is said: "May we (by propitiating Indra) conquer the ill-speaking man."[3]

From the Satapatha Brāhmana, we find that "The Asuras, being deprived of speech, were undone, crying, 'He lava,' 'He lava.' Such was the unintelligible speech which they uttered. And he who speaks thus is a Mlecha. Hence, let no Brāhman speak barbarous language, since such is the speech of the Asuras."[4]

[1] Muir, O.S.T., ii. 49. [2] Ib. ii. 277.

[3] Rig Veda, Wilson, VII. xviii. 13.

[4] Satapatha Br. iii. 2, 1, 23.

We learn from Manu, that those tribes who are outside of the classes produced from the mouth, arms, thighs, and feet of Brāhman, whether they speak the language of the Mlechas or of the Aryas, are called Dasyus."[1] In the time of Manu, therefore, the Aryan language and that of the Mlechas, or Asuras, were both in use. At the period described in the Mahābhārata, however, the Asura language must have almost died out amongst the Aryanized tribes; as Vidura "addressed Yudishthra in the Mlecha tongue, so as to be unintelligible to all except Yudishthra."[2]

At a later period than this, however, the grammarian Rāma Tarkavagisa refers to "those who speak like Nāgas."[3] It would seem, therefore, that the unregenerate Asuras retained the language, as well as the religion and customs, of their forefathers long after their converted brethren had discarded them. It was evidently amongst these unregenerate tribes that the Paisāchi dialects were in use; and amongst these tribes, as we have just seen, were the Dravidian Pāndyas.[4]

This view, that the Tamil and cognate tongues were founded upon the ancient Asura speech, is

[1] Manu, Haughton, x. 45.

[2] Mahābhārata, Adi, Jatagriha, p. cxlvii.

[3] Muir, O.S.T., ii. 52.

[4] Ib. 49.

very strongly confirmed by the fact that the language of the Brahūis, a tribe on the borders of Sind, has been found to be very closely allied to them. Indeed, Dr. Caldwell says: "The Brahūi (language) enables us to trace the Dravidian race, beyond the Indus, to the southern confines of Central Asia."[1] This country, as I have already pointed out, was the home of the Asuras or Nāgas, to which race apparently belonged the founders of the Dravidian kingdoms.

Taking into consideration all the evidence which has been brought forward, the only possible conclusion seems to be, that the Dravidians, of the south of India, were of the same stock as the Asuras or Nāgas of the north.

[1] Grammar of Drav. Lang. Intro., 44.

CHAPTER VIII

THE civilization of Burmah, and other Indo-Chinese countries, is ascribed by legend and by the native historians to invaders from India. And these are connected with the Nāga people of Magadha, and of the north and west of India.

The ancient navigators, too, who carried the Brahmanical and Buddhist religions, the worship of the Nāga, and the Sanscrit or Pāli language to Java, Sumatra, and even to distant Celebes, were Indian people. And they were, doubtless, descendants of those Asura dwellers in the ocean, which are mentioned in the Mahābhārata, and have been already referred to.

From Tamralipti, now Tamlūk, and from other ports on the Bay of Bengal, adventurers, both military and mercantile, found their way to Burmah and the countries beyond. That many, if not most, of these were of Nāga race is shown by the traditions which refer to them, and by the sculptured remains which they have left behind.

We learn from the Mahārājaweng that, before the birth of Buddha, Abhi raja left Kapilavastu and settled in Burmah; that he was succeeded by his son Kan Rajagyi; and that the dynasty was overthrown by invaders from Tsin.[1] The king fled to Malé, where he died, and his queen then married Daza raja, who came from India, and who founded the city of Pagan.[2]

The names of the River Irawadi (Irāvati), of the country of Kambodia (Kambōja), and of several ancient cities in Burmah and Siam, are of Indian origin. And Nākhonvat, the name given to the great serpent temple in Kambodia, is but a corruption of Nāgavaṭi.

It is possible that the Buddhist missionaries, sent to these countries by Asoka, owed much of their success to the good offices of their country-men, already settled there. The islands of the Indo-Chinese Archipelago appear to have been colonized, to a great extent, from western India. Here, too, the earlier adventurers seem to have been worshippers of the sun and the serpent.

In the Island of Bali, near Java, in which the Hindu religion still exists, we find the river Sindhu and the district of Bāsuki (Vāsuki).[3] In this island, which was doubtless named after the great Daitya raja of Pātala, some of the temples contain images of Vāsuki, the Nāga demi-god;

[1] Phayre, Hist. Burmah, 7.
[2] Ib. 9. ff.
[3] J.R.A.S., N.S., ix. 69.

and others those of Garuda and other Hindu deities.[1]

The ritual at the Nāga and Deva temples appears to be much the same as that in use in the Himālaya, which has already been described. At these temples, too, we find the inspired prophet, here called Manku, who is not of Brāhman caste, and who is the mouthpiece of the deity.[2] There are, however, other temples, the priests of which are Brāhmans, and at these the ceremonial more resembles that of orthodox Brahmanical temples in India.

In the island of Bali, at the funeral ceremonies of a man of Kshatriya caste, a representation of a serpent, which is called Nāga, is carried in the procession and is burned with the corpse.[3] In all these countries it was the Nāga or hooded serpent which was held sacred, and it was called by its Indian name.

Another proof, of the ancient connection of these islands with India, is that the Javan era is the Sāka-kala, which is so well known, and is still in use in parts of Western India and in the Himālaya. According to a Javan tradition an expedition from India, led by a son of the king of Kujrat (Gujrat), arrived on the west coast of the

[1] J.R.A.S., N.S., ix. 82.

[2] Ib. ix. 80.

[3] Ib. ix. 95.

island about A.D. 603. A settlement was founded, and the town of Mendan Kamalan was built. Other Hindus followed, and a great trade was established with the ports of India and other countries.[1] There is, however, no reason to suppose that this was the first arrival of Indian voyagers in the Archipelago.

Traditions still remain in western India of expeditions to Java. A Guzerati proverb runs thus: "He who goes to Java never comes back; but if he does return, his descendants, for seven generations, live at ease."[2] The bards in Marwar have a legend that Bhōj raja, the great Puār chief of Ujaini, in anger drove away his son Chandrabhān, who sailed to Java.[3]

Evidence brought forward by Mr. Kennedy[4] shows that a great seaborne trade was carried on from Indian ports by Dravidian merchants as early as the seventh century B.C. The beginnings of Dravidian navigation, however, were probably much earlier than this.

We have seen that the seaborne commerce of the Solar or Nāga tribes of western India had become important at a very early period. Of this the legend of "the churning of the ocean" already

[1] Raffles, Hist. Java, ii. 83.
[2] Bombay Gazetteer, i. 402.
[3] Ib. i. 448.
[4] J.R.A.S., April, 1898.

referred to is an allegorical description, but we have no detailed accounts of ocean voyages until a much later period. Sakya Buddha himself, however, refers to such voyages. He says: "Long ago, ocean-going merchants were wont to plunge forth upon the sea, taking with them a shore-sighting bird. When the ship was out of sight of land, they would set the shore-sighting bird free. And it would go to the east and to the south, and to the west and to the north, and to the intermediate points, and rise aloft. If on the horizon it caught sight of land, thither it would go. But if not, then it would come back to the ship again." [1]

It will be observed that this mode of finding the position of a ship at sea, which recalls the sending out of the birds from the Ark, is said to have been the custom "long ago." It would seem, therefore, that in the fifth century B.C. other and probably more scientific methods were in use. It would also appear that the navigation of the ocean was even then an ancient institution.

In the time of the Chinese Buddhist pilgrim Fah Hian (about 406 A.D.), there was a regular and evidently old-established trade between India and China, and with the islands of the Archipelago.

Fah Hian sailed from Tamalitti, or Tamralipti, at the mouth of the Ganges, in a great merchant

[1] Rhys Davids, J.R.A.S., April, 1899, 432.

ship, and in fourteen days reached Ceylon.[1] From thence he sailed in a great ship, which carried about two hundred men, and which was navigated by observing the sun, moon, and stars. In this ship Fah Hian reached Ye-po-ti (probably Java), in which country heretics and Brāhmans flourished, but the law of Buddha was not much known.[2] Here the pilgrim embarked for China on board another ship carrying two hundred men, amongst whom were Brahmans. These proposed to treat the sramana as Jonah was treated, and for the same reason, but some of those on board took his part. At length, when their provisions were nearly exhausted, they reached China.[3] All these ships appear to have been Indian, and not Chinese.

Fah Hian mentions that pirates were numerous in those seas,[4] which shows that the commerce must have been considerable.

[1] Fo-Kwo-ki, Beal, I. lxxi., lxxii.
[2] Ib. I. lxxx.
[3] Ib. I. lxxxi., lxxxii.
[4] Ib. I. lxxx.

CHAPTER IX

AS already mentioned, both the Buddhist and the Jaina religious systems were closely connected with the worship of the Sun and the serpent. The cause of this appears to have been that each of these forms of religion arose, or at all events found their chief supporters, amongst the Solar tribes who had not come completely under Brahmanical influence. According to Brahmanic authorities, both Buddhism and Jainism had their origin amongst the Asuras. It is said that, when the Devas were defeated by the Daityas, under Hrada son of Hiranyakasipu, they appealed to Vishnu.[1] That deity heard their prayers, and promised to assist them. To this end he sent a great delusion, in the shape of a naked mendicant, with head shaven and with a bunch of peacock's feathers in his hand, to delude the Daityas; who, being thus seduced from the religion of the Vedas, were called Arhatas."[2]

Now the Jainas were naked ascetics, who were called Arhatas, and they are evidently here alluded

[1] Vishnu Purāna, III. xviii. 325.
[2] Ib. III. xviii. 337, 339.

to. But, in addition to this, we are told that the same deluder, putting on garments of a red colour, assumed a benevolent aspect, and speaking in soft and agreeable tones, addressed others of the Daitya family ; and these were induced to deviate from their religious duties, and become Bauddhas[1] (Buddhists). It is further said, that the Daityas became perverted, so that not one of them admitted the authority of the Vedas.[2]

In the passages just quoted, the original Digambara Jainas are evidently referred to. There is no mention of the later Swetambara, or white-robed sect. The legend, therefore, must be an early one. Religious asceticism appears to have been a very ancient institution in India. We are told, on Brahmanical authority, of rajas who in early times, resigned the sovereignty to their sons and retired to the forest to lead a life of ascetism. Thus Agnidhra, grandson of Manu, his son Nābhi, Rishaba son of Nābhi, and his son Bhārata are all said to have resigned their thrones and become hermits.[3] Of these Rishaba is called an Arhat,[4] and is said to have died naked.[5] He, and Sumati his grandson, are claimed, by the Jainas, as Tirthakaras, or deified anchorets of that sect.[6]

[1] Vishnu Purāna, III. xviii. 340, 341. [2] Ib.
[3] Vishnu Purāna, Wilson, II. i. 162, 164.
[4] Gaina Sutras, Jacobi, 281.
[5] Vishnu Purāna, II. i. 163. [6] Gaina Sutras, 280, 282.

We learn also from Brahmanical sources, that some devotees, belonging to royal houses, gave up, like Sakya Buddha, their right of succession to the throne of their fathers, to lead a life of asceticism. Yāti, son of Yayāti and brother of Nahush, who refused to reign, "and became a mūni, like unto Brahma himself";[1] and Devapi son of Pratipa, whe gave up the throne to his younger brother Santanu, and became a hermit,[2] are notable examples.

The term Yāti is still applied to Jaina devotees.

The Siddhas, who are associated as divine beings with the Devas and the Nāgas, appear to have been deified mūnis or ascetics. Of these Kapila, Vyasa, Vashista, Visvamitra, and Baradhwaja, are mentioned by name, as entitled to worship with oblations.[3] The Siddhas, thus, must at that time have included both Brahmans and Kshatriyas.

In the Baghavad Gita, Krishna says: "Amongst Siddhas, I am Kapila Mūni." Now Kapila Mūni appears to have been the same with Kapila king of the Nāgas, whose tirtha at Kapilavastu was a sacred place of pilgrimage before the great war of the Mahābhārata;[4] and evidently before the

[1] Mahābhārata, Adi, Sambhava, p. lxxv.

[2] Ib. xcv.

[3] Asvalayana Grihya Sutra, iii. 4, 1 (S.B.E.)

[4] Mahābhārata, Vana, Tirthayatra, p. lxxxiv.

time of Krishna. It is very unlikely that Krishna would have compared himself with Kapila Mūni had that ascetic not been very eminent amongst the Siddhas. This Muni, however, had been king of the Nāgas of Pātala; and was therefore an Asura and a Nāga.

A Kapila, probably the same, is mentioned amongst the Dānavas.[1] Whether this was Kapila Mūni or not, however, we find that "Kapila, the most righteous of saints, he whom the great saints name as Kapila Vāsudeva,"[2] ruled over the Nāgas in Pātala, and destroyed the 60,000 sons of Sagara when they invaded his dominions.[3]

The emblem of the Siddhas, as now worshipped, is a pair of human feet, carved upon a stone tablet, or upon a rock. Sometimes, between the feet, there is a representation of the short crutch used by religious devotees, to lean upon, while engaged in meditation. The Siddh-pat, as this foot emblem is called, is a common object of worship in the Kangra valley, and in other districts bordering upon the Himālaya.

Offerings of fruit, flowers, and grain, are made to the Siddhas; but animals are not sacrificed to them, nor is dancing or music usually connected with their worship. Like other divinities,

[1] Vishnu Purāna, I. xxi. 147.
[2] Mahābhārata, Vana, Tirthayatra, p. cvii.
[3] Vishnu Purāna, IV. iv. 378.

they receive votive offerings. These generally take the shape of small wooden imitations of human feet, or sandals. In some places the Siddhas are represented by a plain rounded stone, or pinda, set up under a tree. This is marked with white, instead of the red colouring applied to the symbols of most other deities.

Pilgrimages are made to the shrines of the Siddhas, and the pilgrim's mark, or "Likhnu," is a rude representation of a pair of human feet. The Siddhas are often worshipped as household gods.

The foot-emblem seems to be very ancient. It is, in fact, a form of memorial of the dead. Hence, probably, it was adopted by the followers of Buddha, in remembrance of their great leader.

In the Himālaya, when a bridge over a stream, or a resting-place for travellers is erected, in memory of some wealthy villager, the imitation of a pair of human feet is carved upon it. This is supposed to represent the footprints of the deceased, just as the post, with a human head carved upon it, personifies the living donor of a similar gift for the public benefit.

The footprints are still used as memorials of religious devotees. At the village of Dosun, in the upper Sutlej valley, is a shrine dedicated to Gobind, the great Gūru of the Sikhs, who is represented by a stone tablet, with a pair of human feet carved upon it.

RUINED TEMPLE OF SIDDH-NATH,
KANGRA VALLEY.

The Jainas, who, as we have just seen, are said by Brahmanical writers to have been Asuras, applied the term Siddha to their deified ascetics. Of the twenty-four Tirthakaras, or deified anchorites of the Jainas, all were Kshatriyas, and twenty-two of them were of the Solar race of Ikshvāku.[1] No wonder, then, that they were closely connected with the Sun and the serpent. The last of the Tirthakaras, Vardhamana or Mahābir, was a contemporary of Sakya Buddha. He was the son of Siddartha, raja of Konigamma, near Vaisāli, and was related by marriage to Bimbisaro, raja of Maghada.[2] By permission of his elder brother, Vardhamana became an ascetic; after one year he went naked; after twelve years he became a Jina or Tirthakara, and was called Mahābir.[3] After his death, he became a Siddha.[4] Parswa, the Tirthakara who preceded Mahābir, was a son of Aswasena, raja of Benares.[5] He is always represented with the seven hoods of a Nāga expanded over his head. Fergusson found the serpent in all the Jaina temples at Abu.[6] And the colossal Jaina statues, at Sravana Belgola

[1] Gaina Sutras, Jaçobi, 218.
[2] Ib. Intro. x.–xiv.
[3] Gaina Sutras, Jacobi, xv.
[4] Ib. 264.
[5] Ib. 271.
[6] "Tree and Serpent Worship," 73.

and at Yannur, in southern India, have Nāgas in attendance.[1]

That Buddha, and the Buddhist religion, were intimately connected with serpent-worship has often been noticed. Indeed all interested in the subject may convince themselves, of this close relationship, by a study of Fergusson's beautiful photographs of the Amrāvati sculptures, or by an examination of the sculptures themselves at the British Museum.

Sakya Buddha was of Solar race and a descendant of Ikshvāku. At the commencement of his religious career he was sheltered and protected by the Nāga raja Muchalinda.[2] Throughout his life he was on friendly terms with the Nāga people. And, at his death, Nāga rajas claimed to share his relics, and built stupas over them.[3]

How close was the connexion between Buddhism and these descendants of the Asuras, we may see from the Amrāvati, Sanchi, and other sculptures. In these the Nāga people are shown as engaged in adoration of Buddha, or Buddhist emblems;[4] and in some instances these emblems are represented as being worshipped in the same temple as

[1] "Indian and Eastern Architecture," 269.
Sravana Belgola, Rice, 29.

[2] Mahāvagga (S.B.E.), i. 3, 2; Hiouen Tsiang, Beal, ii. 41.

[3] Hiouen Tsiang, ii. 128.

[4] "Tree and Serpent Worship," plates lxx., lxxii.
B. Museum No. 8; J.R.A.S., April, 1899, 422.

the Nāga.[1] The serpent, in several of the Amrāvati sculptures, occupies the place of honour in the dagoba, which is usually assigned to Buddha himself.[2] And in some of them, Buddha is shown as having his head sheltered by the expanded hoods of a seven-headed Nāga,[3] which was, as we have seen, the distinctive mark of a Nāga raja.

The Sun, the Trisul, and other Solar emblems, are also represented, in the bas-reliefs from Amrāvati, as objects of Buddhist worship.

Even in the time of the Chinese pilgrims, we find Buddhist sramanas worshipping the Nāga, and conducting the rites at Nāga temples.[4]

In addition to what has already been said, we find that Buddha was addressed by his followers as Mahānāgo, or great Nāga.[5]

It is not difficult to explain all this, for we learn from Brahmanical and from Buddhist authorities, that the tribe to which Buddha belonged was of Solar race. The Sakyas were descendants of Ikshvāku, the raja of Pātala.[6] Sakya, too, his

[1] "Tree and Serpent Worship," plate lxx.

[2] B. Museum Nos. 45, 74, 81, 89.

[3] B. Museum No. 72.

[4] Fah Hian, Beal, I. xli.
Hiouen Tsiang, i. 137.

[5] Pāryānavagga (S.B.E.), 195.

[6] Rockhill, 12, Mahāwanso, Turnour, xxxv. Lal. Vist. ii. 140.

father Suddhodana, and his son Rahula, are said in the Purānas to be of the race of Ikshvāku.[1]

According to Buddhist records, one of the kings of Pātala, of this race, having promised the succession to the throne to a younger son, by a favourite wife, sent away his elder sons to provide for themselves. These, in the course of their travels, came to Kapilavastu.[2] Here was the tirtha or shrine of the great ascetic Kapila Mūni; who had been, as we have already seen, king of the Nāgas of Pātala,[3] and was doubtless an ancestral deity. The sons of the King of Pātala settled at Kapilavastu, and their descendants remained in possession until the time of Buddha. The city was then destroyed by Virudhaka raja; and, with the exception of Buddha and four others, all the Sakyas were destroyed. One of those who escaped became raja of Udyāna, and married a Nāga princess, over whose head appeared the nine hoods of a serpent.[4] This Sakya chief of Udyāna, Uttara Sena, who has already been referred to, received a share of the relics of Buddha, over which he built a stupa.[5]

[1] Vishnu Purāna, IV. xxii. 463.

[2] Mahāwanso, Turnour, Int. xxxv., Rockhill, 12, Lal. Vist. ii. 140.

[3] Mahābhārata, Vana, Tirthayatra, p. lxxxiv.

[4] Hiouen Tsiang, Beal, i. 132, ii. 20.

[5] Ib. i. 132.

This evidence, that Buddha and the Sakyas were of Nāga, or Solar, race, was confirmed in a remarkable manner lately. In 1898 the stupas erected over the relics of the Sakyas, who were killed when Kapilavastu was destroyed by the king of Magadha, were opened; and in nearly every relic casket was found the representation of a Nāga. One of these caskets, which contained a golden Nāga, bore the name of Mahānāman, one of Buddha's own family, who succeeded to the throne, which would have been inherited by Gautama himself, had he not renounced the world.[1]

[1] Ind. Arch. Reports, N.W.P., 1898.

CHAPTER X

IN the foregoing pages it has been shown that, in India, the hooded serpent, that is the Nàga or Cobra, was always associated with the worship of the Sun; and that it was held sacred, as the protector, or totem, of a race which claimed descent from the Sun-god.

It has also been shown that the chiefs of the Solar race were, after death, worshipped as gods or demi-gods; and that these demi-gods were usually represented with the hoods of protecting serpents expanded over their heads.

It has been pointed out, too, that these deified chiefs were the Nāgas of Swarga (Indra's heaven), and of the epic poems; the celestial serpents belonging to Sūrya (the Sun), of the Brahmanical writers; and the Nāga rajas of Indian folk-lore.

In addition to this, we have seen that many of the Solar kings, especially those who claimed paramount power, received divine honours, while living, as incarnations of the Sun-god; and that, in this capacity, they were believed to have con-

SHRINE OF BRIHĀRU NĀG,
SARĀJ
(showing post with Chakra of Sun).

trol over the elements, and other supernatural powers.

It has been shown that, in order to obtain the favour of the serpent deities, sacrifices were offered to them; and that many of the victims, so offered, were human beings.

Serpent-worship, however, was not confined to India, although its birthplace appears to have been in Asia.

Wherever the Sun was worshipped, and the people or their rulers claimed descent from the Sun-god, there the hooded-serpent was held sacred.

As in India, so too in other countries, the serpent was worshipped as the protector, or totem, of people who claimed Solar descent. Moreover, the worship of the Sun and the serpent was everywhere conducted with the same, or almost the same, rites and ceremonial as those now, or formerly, existing in India.

It seems in the highest degree improbable that this close connexion between the Sun and the serpent could have originated, independently, in countries so far apart as China and the west of Africa, or India and Peru. And it seems scarcely possible that, in addition to this, the same forms of worship of these deities, and the same ritual, could have arisen, spontaneously, amongst each of these far distant peoples. The alternative appears to be, that the combined worship of the Sun and the serpent-gods must have spread from a common centre, by the migration of, or communication with, the people who claimed Solar descent.

So universally was the Nāga held sacred, that it would seem to have been the earliest totem of the people who claimed descent from the Sun-god.

The tortoise, too, was a very ancient totem of the Solar race. Like the hooded serpent, it is held sacred in many different countries, and is always associated with the Sun.

The worship of the Sun and the serpent is found already existing, and indeed fully developed, at the earliest dawn of history. No attempt will be made, here, to trace its spread throughout the ancient world; but in many countries, besides India, it still remains, or has left its trace behind, and some of these will be briefly referred to.

The existence of Sun and serpent worship at a very remote period, in the countries between the Euphrates and the Indus, has already been alluded to. The conflicts between the Āryans and the serpent race of Ahi, as described in the Veda, and the struggles between the Iranians and the dynasty of Azi dahāka, in the same region, as recounted by Persian writers, have also been mentioned.

In these, its ancient seats, traces of the worship of the Sun and the serpent still remain. The

Yezidis, or so-called "devil-worshippers," of the Zagros mountains, who are probably a remnant of the ancient Medic or Proto-medic inhabitants, still worship the Sun-god;[1] still pray towards the rising Sun; and still have the serpent carved upon their sacred buildings.[2]

Although many modifications occurred in later times, it is probable that, in the very early days of Babylonia, the worship of the Sun and the serpent was the form of religion which prevailed there and in the adjacent countries.

One of the earliest of the gods of Babylonia was Ea, whose emblem was the seven-headed serpent,[3] and who was the god of the river of the great serpent, or the Euphrates.[4]

Amongst the Chaldeans, Hea, or Ea, and his son Marduk, were the deities invoked for protection from all infernal powers, and from sorcery,[5] in fact, from perils of every kind. Ea was the god of wisdom. In the Chaldean account of the Deluge, it is said that Ea gave warning of the coming flood, and directed the preparation of the ark or ship. It is also said that Ea declared this to his minister, who heard and proclaimed the

[1] Layard, Nineveh, i. 289, 290. Ragozin, Media, 270.
[2] Layard, Nineveh, i. 283, 301.
[3] Budge, Bab. Life and Hist., 132. Chaldean Magic, 232.
[4] Sayce, Hibbert Lecture, 134.
[5] Chaldean Magic, iv. 59.

commands to Adrakhasis, the man of Surippak,[1] who was the Chaldean Noah.

The worship of Ea seems to have been widely spread. In a letter, sent by Dusratta, King of Mittani, to Amenophis III, King of Egypt, in which several deities are invoked, the god Ea is said to be "Lord of all."[2]

The hooded serpent does not seem to have been a totem of the Semites. It appears to have been taken over, by the Babylonians, with the ancient religion of Accad, or of Sumer. It was not adopted by the Hebrews, with whom, except in one well-known instance, the serpent was the personification of evil. It was, in Babylonia, still connected with the Sun, even in later days, for Nebuchadrezzar tells us that he set up images, of poisonous snakes, at the gates of the great temple of Marduk, the Sun-god of Babylon.[3]

The Sun, under different names, and the serpent gods, were probably the chief deities of all the Turanian tribes, who occupied the country to the south and west of the Kaspian. We are told that in Sākadwipa, Vishnu was worshipped as the Sun.[4]

It may be noted that Suriash, the name of the Kassite Sun-god,[5] closely resembles that of Sūrya,

[1] Chaldean Account of Genesis, 279, 280.

[2] Conder, J.R.A.S., Oct., 1892.

[3] Budge, Bab. Life and Hist., i. 17.

[4] Vishnu Purāna, II. iv. 200.

[5] "Struggle of Nations," 115.

one of the names of the Sun-god of the Hindus.

A deity named Suriha, too, is referred to in Assyrian inscriptions and is apparently the same as Aa or Ea,[1] who, as we have just seen, was father of Marduk the Sun-god of Babylon, and perhaps was, originally, the Sun-god himself. Probably, too, he was the same as the Indian Vishnu.

The ancient Chaldean epic poem, of which Izdubar or Gilgames is the hero,[2] throws much light upon the religion of Elam and the neighbouring countries at a very early period; and enables us to see how closely the Sun and serpent worship of India was related to it.

We learn from the poem that Khambaba, King of Elam, had invaded Chaldea and laid waste the country of the Euphrates.[3] Gilgames, who was King of Uruk or Erech,[4] with Eabani, who was probably the chief of some neighbouring pastoral tribe, made a raid into Elam. They surprised and killed Khambaba, at the sanctuary of Irnini, on "the hill of cedars, the abode of the gods."[5] The heroes greatly admired the grandeur of the sacred cedars, in the dominions of Khambaba.

On his victorious return to Uruk, Gilgames offended the goddess Ishtar, by whom he was

[1] Pinches, "Review of John's Assryrian Deeds," J.R.A.S., July, 1902, 685.

[2] Maspero, "Dawn of Civilization," 574.

[3] Ib. 579. [4] Ib. 574. [5] Ib. 579.

cursed, and afflicted with a skin disease.[1] To obtain relief from this malady, the hero made a pilgrimage to the abode (or shrine) of his deified ancestor Adrakhasis, or Shamash-napishtim, or Utu-napishtim, who had been King of Shurippak; who had been saved in the ark at the time of the deluge[2]; and who has been already alluded to.

The pilgrimage was made partly by land, and partly by sea, or by river.

Gilgames having, by the advice of his ancestor, bathed in a sacred water, was cured; and he received from Samash-napishtim, or perhaps from the priest of his temple, a branch of the tree of life.[3]

On his way home, Gilgames landed upon the shore of what seems to have been a hostile country; and while he was drinking at a spring, the branch of the tree of life was seized by a serpent, who was the genius (or deity) of the spring. The serpent, uttering a malediction, carried off the branch; and Gilgames, who was unable to recover it, and was much distressed at his loss, resumed his homeward journey.[4]

It is evident, from this description, that in some of the countries bordering upon the Persian Gulf, springs were, as in India, sacred to the serpent-

[1] Maspero, "Dawn of Civilization," 582.
[2] Chaldean "Account of Genesis," 288.
Maspero, "Dawn of Civilization," 566.
[3] Ib. 587. [4] Ib. 587–588.

TEMPLE OF DEVI AT BARMAOR
Decorated with horns of Ibex.

gods; and this in very early times. The Chaldean epic is supposed to date from about 2000 B.C.,[1] but the events referred to had occurred long before.

Several of the religious customs mentioned in the Chaldean poem, such as pilgrimages to the shrines of deified ancestors, the temples being sheltered in groves of cedar, and their being decorated with the horns of animals killed in the chase, exist to this day, amongst the worshippers of the Sun and the serpent in the Himālaya.

Gilgames was at first an ordinary mortal, but he appears to have become a god, and his mother is called a goddess.[2] He seems in fact to have become a personification of the Sun-god. Possibly, like so many other Solar chiefs, Gilgames assumed divine honours, as an incarnation of that deïty, upon attaining to sovereign power. A tablet has been found containing prayers addressed to him as a god.[3]

Khambaba also, the King of Elam who was killed by Gilgames, seems to have been a personification of the Sun-god.[4]

It may be noted that Gilgames, as represented in Chaldean sculpture, with his broad and bearded

[1] "Chaldean Account of Genesis," 178.

[2] "Dawn of Civilization," 574.

[3] "Chaldean Account of Genesis," 176, 179. "Dawn of Civilization," 574, 575.

[4] "Chaldean Account of Genesis," 225.

face, and his long and curling locks, much resembled a Brahūi or Balūch chief of the present day.

What appears to be another link, connecting the Indian branch of the Solar race with the countries to the southward of the Kaspian, is the tradition of the deluge. This is recorded, with some variations, in the Satapatha Brāhmana, the Mahābhārata, and the Purānas. The legend was probably brought by the Asuras from their original home.

It is noteworthy that the warning of the coming flood was given, not to the rishis, nor to the Brahmans, but to Manu, a Kshatriya chief, son of the Sun, and progenitor of Ikshvāku and the Indian branch of the Solar race.

In all the Indian versions, the part taken by the fish, in warning Manu, or Vaivaswat, or Satyavrata, of the approaching flood, and in directing the building of the ship or ark, greatly resembles that ascribed to the god Ea, in the Chaldean account of the same event. This deity, moreover, is represented as sometimes taking the form of a fish, though, at other times, his emblem was the seven-headed serpent.

In the earliest version of the Indian legend, which is that of the Satapatha Brāhmana, no locality is mentioned. It is said that, as Manu was performing his morning ablutions, a fish came into his hands. The fish said: "Rear me. I will save thee. A flood will carry away all these creatures." Manu placed the fish in a jar; when it grew larger, he removed it to a pond; when it grew still larger, he placed it in the sea. The fish then told Manu to prepare a ship, and, when the flood rose, to go into it. Manu did as he was directed, and when the deluge came, he embarked in the ship. The fish came to him, and, to a horn upon its head, Manu tied a rope, by which the ship was towed through the flood to the northern mountain. The fish then said—"I have saved thee," and directed Manu to fasten the ship to a tree.[1]

In the Mahābhārata, the legend assumes a more local character. Manu Vaivaswat is there said to have been engaged in religious asceticism in the forest of Visālā, when a fish came to the bank of the river, and begged for protection from the other fishes. Visālā, as we have already seen, was a city of Takshaka Vaisālya, the Nāga chief.[2]

Manu took the fish out of the water, and placed it in a jar; removing it, as it grew, to a pond, to the river, and finally to the sea. The fish then foretold the destruction of all creatures on earth, by a flood, and directed Manu to build a strong ark, or ship, furnished with a long rope, saying—

[1] Satapatha Brāhmana, i. viii. i. (S.B.E. xii.)

[2] Ante, p. 106.

"Without my help thou canst not save thyself from this fearful flood."[1]

Manu embarked, with the seven rishis, and all the different kinds of seeds, and the ark was taken by the fish to the Himāvat, where it was tied to a tree. The fish then, addressing the rishis, said—"I am Brahmā, the lord of all creatures; there is none greater than myself; assuming the form of a fish, I have saved you from this destruction."[2]

In the Bhāgavata Purāna, the legend is localized in southern India. Manu, or Satyavrata, is there called "the lord of Dravida," and the fish comes into his hands, as he is offering an oblation of water in the river Kritamala,[3] which is said to rise in the hills of Malaya or Malabar.[4]

Thus we see that it is in the later versions of the legend only that the event is said to have occurred in India; and in them it is referred to different localities.

No doubt both the Chaldean epic and the Indian legend refer to the same flood, and probably the Chinese tradition does so too.

In some versions of the Hindu account of the deluge, the fish which saved Manu is said to have been a manifestation of Vishnu. In connexion

[1] Mahābhārata, Vana, p. clxxxvii.
[2] Ib.
[3] Muir, O.S.T., i. 209.
[4] Vishnu Purāna, II. iii. 176.

with this, it may be noted that both the Babylonian Hea and the Indian Vishnu were associated with the sea, the fish, and the many-headed serpent. May they not have been the same deity under different names? Fish are held sacred in many parts of India, and are especially connected with Vishnu.

CHAPTER XI

THE Sun and the Serpent were worshipped by the Phœnicians. They probably derived the cult from Babylonia, and they no doubt carried it into other countries, as is shown by the legend of Cadmus. The Phœnicians also worshipped many other deities, some of which were doubtless of Babylonian origin.

Traces of Sun and Serpent worship remained in Syria and other parts of western Asia down to, and even after, the introduction of Christianity. Indeed this ancient form of religion was curiously blended with the ritual of some of the early Christian, or rather semi-Christian sects, such as the Gnostics.

Several centuries after the Christian era, some of the Gnostics actually worshipped the serpent.[1]

The Manichæans, too, seem to have borrowed largely from the old Sun and Serpent worship. In prayer they turned towards the Sun.[2] According to them, Christ dwelt in the Sun, came from

[1] Irenæus, i. 30; Moeller, i. 136; Mosheim, Inst. Eccles. Hist. v. 81.

[2] Aug. c. Fortunatum, 3; Robertson, Hist. Ch. Ch. vii. 199.

thence, to sojourn upon the earth, and afterwards returned there.[1] They also held the Serpent to be a beneficent agent.[2]

The legend of St. George and the dragon, although it assumed its present shape in Christian times, was probably founded upon an older story.

The Greeks worshipped the Sun and the Serpent from a very early period of their history. Cecrops, the first King of Athens, is said to have come from Egypt, and to have been half man and half serpent.[3] He and his successors were deified. Cadmus too, the Phœnician founder of Thebes, and his wife Harmonia are said to have been transformed into serpents.[4]

Cadmus, on his arrival in Greece, found serpent tribes already in possession of the country, or at all events of part of it.

Several writers mention that, on arriving in Bœotia, the Phœnician chief, in obedience to an oracle, resolved to found a city. On searching for water, he found a spring, which was guarded by a great serpent, who killed all those who came near. Cadmus, however, killed the serpent, and built the city of Thebes.[5]

[1] Mosheim, Inst. Eccles. Hist., v. 109.
[2] Neander, ii. 183; Robertson, Hist. Ch. Ch., vii. 193.
[3] Bryant ii. 210. [4] Strabo, Geog., I. ii. 39.
[5] Lenormant, "Légende de Cadmus," 5.

The Sun and Serpent worship of Greece, in historic times, was mixed up with the worship of many other deities, as was that of Semitic Babylonia, in which country some of these Grecian deities seem to have had their origin.

The serpent, in Greece, held a somewhat subordinate position, and was not so distinctly connected with the Sun as in Egypt, India, and other countries, in which it was the totem of the dominant Solar race. Still, even in Greece, the Serpent was considered as a protector. The guardian deity of the Athenian Acropolis was a great serpent.[1]

The worship of the Sun and the Serpent has left its traces in nearly every part of Europe. Its spread was probably due in part to the Egyptians, and in part to the Phœnicians; but its progress westward seems to have been largely owing to the migration of other peoples, who were apparently of Asiatic origin.

In Egypt, the Sun was worshipped, and the Ureus or hooded serpent was held sacred, from the earliest times of which any knowledge exists; although modifications were introduced under different dynasties.

The Pharaohs claimed descent from the Sun. Each reigning king was considered as an incarnation of the Sun-god and, as such, received divine

[1] Herodotus, Urania, xli.

honours while living. Each had his temples, in which his statue sat enthroned, received worship, delivered oracles, and fulfilled all the functions of a divine being.[1]

The Pharaohs, as already mentioned, were addressed officially as "The King, My Lord, My Sun-god." This form of address was used by the Egyptian governors of provinces, when sending their reports to the King.[2]

After death, each Pharaoh was worshipped as a deity.

A representation of the hooded serpent was attached to the front of the King's head-dress. This was not merely a badge of royalty, but was also a protector; and was supposed to be able to destroy those who should dare to attack the Pharaoh.[3]

In Egypt, the Sun and the serpent were as closely connected as in other countries, whose rulers claimed Solar descent. In a Theban papyrus, dedicated to Harmakhis, the Sun is described as standing in his divine bark, with the coils of the serpent (Ureus) around him.[4]

The social customs and religious rites of the Egyptians were closely related to those of the

[1] Maspero, "Dawn of Civilization," 266.
[2] "Records of Past," N.S., v. 77, 78, 79, 95.
[3] "Dawn of Civilization," 265.
[4] Maspero, "Struggle of the Nations," 496.

sun-worshipping people of Asia. There can, indeed, be little doubt as to the Asiatic origin of the Pharaohs and their followers.

The various animals, worshipped by the ancient Egyptians, were doubtless originally totems.

The Ethiopians, or Abyssinians, before their conversion to Christianity, were worshippers of the Sun and the Serpent. The Ethiopian king, when at Heliopolis, acted as priest at the temple of the Sun.[1]

Like the Pharaohs, and other chiefs of Solar race, the Ethiopian kings received divine honours.[2]

By the Egyptians, the Ethiopians were called Kaushu or Kush, which recalls the Kashshu, or Kassites of the country to the eastward of the Tigris. Indeed the Kaushu have been considered by Lepsius and others to have come from Asia, and to have been related to the races of Elam.[3]

In connexion with this, it may be noted that Negūs, the title of the king of Abyssinia, appears to be closely related to that of Negi, which is borne by chiefs of the serpent-worshipping Khus tribes of the Himālaya.

The country of Pūanit or Pūnt, which adjoined Ethiopia, and which appears to have included

[1] Maspero, " Dawn of Civilization," 125 (note).

[2] Strabo, Geog., XVII. ii. 2.

[3] Maspero, " Dawn of Civilization," 488 (note).

the shores and islands of the Red Sea,[1] was described by the Egyptians as being inhabited by serpents. According to an ancient papyrus, translated by Golenischeff, the chief of Pūanit, who was a great serpent, told an Egyptian shipwrecked mariner that in four months a ship would arrive from his country, and that after a two months' voyage he would reach his home.[2] There must, therefore, have been a regular trade between Egypt and this country of serpents.

In the kingdoms of Western and Central Africa, except where it had been displaced by Mohammedanism, Sun and Serpent worship existed, in a very barbarous form, down to our own times, and is hardly yet extinct. The Ju-Ju or Fetish ceremonies, in these countries, were really the worship of the Sun and the Serpent, and of deified kings and ancestors.[3]

Here the human sacrifices, and other horrors, were on a scale unknown in other parts of the world, except perhaps in Mexico. The serpent, the tortoise, and other totems of the Solar race, were held sacred.[4] No important business was undertaken without a sacrifice to the serpent,

[1] Maspero, "Dawn of Civilization," 397.

[2] Ib. 496, 497, 498.

[3] Ellis, Hist. Gold Coast, 291, 338, 375. Skertchley, Dahomey, 235, 396.

[4] Ib. 314, 315, 316.

which was everywhere a tutelary deity.[1] The cabalistic signs, used by the priests for magical purposes, were, most if not all of them, identical with those in use in India, and in other Sun-worshipping countries of Asia.[2]

How the combination of Sun and Serpent worship reached these countries is uncertain. It seems, however, to have prevailed, before the introduction of Mohammedanism, over a great part of the African continent. There can be little doubt that it came originally from Asia, and did not arise amongst the negro tribes. Some of the minor deities, however, were probably of aboriginal descent.

In China, and the neighbouring countries, the worship of the Sun and the Serpent appears to be the most ancient form of religion of which any memory remains; and it is still widely prevalent. It is associated, as in India and other countries, with the worship of deified ancestors.

The Emperor of China is said to be the son of Heaven, or rather of the supreme deity.[3] He receives divine honours while living, and after death he is worshipped as a god.[4]

The Nāga or dragon still protects the empire,

[1] Skertchley, Dahomey, 466.
[2] Ib. 470, 475, illust.
[3] Legge, Shu King, Pref. xxiv.–xxvi.
[4] Shih King, Odes, p. 304 ff.

as he has done since the earliest period of Chinese history or legend. He controls the elements, and is worshipped officially in times of drought or floods. Shrines to Lung Wang, the Dragon King, or Nāga raja, are numerous.

The tortoise is also sacred, and its shell is consulted as an oracle.[1]

The commander of a Chinese army was distinguished by a tortoise and serpent banner.[2]

According to Chinese historians, some of their early mythological emperors were half man and half serpent.

T'aihao, or Paohsi, or Fushi, had a serpent's body, a man's head, and the virtue of a sage.[3] His successor, Nükua, had the body of a serpent, the head of a man, and the virtue of a holy man.[4]

Another divine king, Shennung, called "the blazing god," was born under the influence of a sacred dragon. He had the body of a man, and the head of an ox, or rather perhaps of a bull.[5]

M. Terrien de Lacouperie held that the civilization of China came from the west; and that it was an offshoot from that very ancient culture, which apparently had its origin in the country between the Kaspian Sea and the Persian Gulf.[6]

[1] Legge, Shu King, x. 120; Shi King, 351 (note).
[2] Ib. 418.
[3] H. I. Allen, J.R.A.S., April, 1894.
[4] Ib.
[5] Ib.
[6] Early Hist. Chinese Civilization, 26, 27.

These views have been accepted by other eminent scholars, though not by all.

We have seen that, from the region just mentioned, came the Dravidian civilization of India, and the worship of the Sun and the Serpent, which was associated with it.

In Manchuria, the people are of Solar race, and the Nāga demi-gods still control the rivers and the rain.[1] The lake, which occupies the crater of the holy "Ever-white Mountain," is sacred to Lung Wang, the dragon king.[2]

In Korea, the kings are descendants of the Sun, and are protected by the dragon. The people feed, venerate, and worship serpents, as the guardian genii of their households.[3] The tortoise too is sacred.

In Japan, the Sun-god seems to have become a goddess. The Mikado is descended, in unbroken line, from the Sun-goddess; and is himself a divine being.[4]

Of the Kami (gods or demi-gods), some were men, some were dragons, and some were other animals.[5] These probably represent ancestors and totems.

[1] James, "The Long White Mountain," 182.
[2] Ib. 263.
[3] Griffis, Korea, 305.
[4] Adams, Hist. Japan, i. 5, i. 11.
[5] Reid, Japan, 1, 40.

According to Japanese annals, deities of the mountains took the form of serpents.[1]

In these countries, the ritual connected with the worship of the Sun and the Serpent was, in all essential particulars, the same as that used in India.

In the early centuries of the Christian era, the Chinese Buddhist pilgrims, on their way to India, found the Nāga demi-gods in possession of all the rivers and lakes in the countries through which they passed.

In Thibet, springs, rivers, and lakes, are still ruled by the Nāga demi-gods, or Lu.[2]

A Nāga king lives in a crystal palace in the depths of lake Palti.

In 1882, the Grand Lama of Tashilunpo, who was ill, having bathed in the hot springs of Barchu-tsan without benefit, it was supposed that the Nāgas must have been offended in some way. In consequence of this, religious services were held, by the lamas, to propitiate the serpent deities.[3]

Thus we find that, in Thibet, the worship of the serpent gods is still conducted by Buddhist priests, as we have seen that it once was in India.

On the American continent, at the time of the

[1] Nihongi, i. 208, i. 298.

[2] Sarat Chandra Das, Tibet, 139, 140.

[3] Ib. 205.

Spanish invasion, Sun and Serpent worship was universal, and the form, in which it existed there, appears to have been exactly the same as that which was once so general in the old world; except that the place of the hooded serpent, which did not exist in America, was taken by the native rattlesnake. This, however, retained all the attributes ascribed in the old world to the Nāga.

In Peru, Pizarro met the Inca Atahualpa at Cassamarca, in the house (or temple) of the serpent, in which was a serpent of stone.[1] The Inca, in choosing this place of meeting, doubtless hoped for the protection of his ancestral deity.

The tortoise, which is so closely connected with the Sun and Serpent worship of the other hemisphere, and which was doubtless one of the earliest totems of the Solar race, was sacred also with the Sun-worshippers of America.

Both the serpent and the tortoise were represented with human heads,[2] which shows that they were worshipped, not as mere reptiles, but as totems. In fact here, as in the old world, they represented the ancestors, as well as the protectors, of the race.

The rites and ceremonial employed in the wor-

[1] Helps, Life of Pizarro, 161.

[2] Kingsborough's Mex. Antiq., vol. iv. pl.

ship of the Sun and the Serpent appear to have been essentially the same in Asia and in America. Moreover, in the new, as in the old world, the people who worshipped the serpent were of Solar race; the kings claimed divine honours, while living, as the Sun-god personified; and after death they were worshipped as deities. The laws, too, and the social and other customs, which were in use in America at the time of its discovery, so greatly resembled those of the Sun-worshipping countries of the old world, that there seems good reason to believe in that Asiatic origin, of the religion and civilization of the Indian nations of America, which has been suggested by several writers. Even the lasso and the scalping-knife appear to have been taken from Asia.[1]

[1] Herodotus, Melpomene, lxiv.; Polymnia, lxxxvi. Shahnāma, Atkinson, 212, 240.

CHAPTER XII

WE have seen that the worship of the Sun and the Serpent was, in times past, well-nigh universal; and that it was already established, amongst some of the most enlightened peoples of antiquity, at the earliest period of which any history has come down to us.

We have seen, also, that the hooded serpent was held sacred as a totem of the people who claimed descent from the Sun-god; and thus came to be worshipped as a deity.

It would seem, moreover, that the deification of totems, of kings, of ancestors, and of the heavenly bodies, which furnished so many of the divinities associated with the Sun-god; as also the human sacrifices and other abominations, which occurred in some Sun-worshipping countries, all arose from the corruption of the earlier worship of a supreme deity who was believed to reside in the Sun.

The Gāyatrī — the most sacred text of the Veda, which must not be uttered so as to be over-heard by profane ears, and which contains the essence of the Hindu religion, is a short prayer to the Sun-god, who is addressed as Savitri, the generator or creator.

The early Egyptians, and other ancient peoples also, seem to have worshipped the Sun-god as the Creator.